A Student's Guide to
Word 6 for Windows
on the IBM PC Compatible

by

Adrian Beck

Mark Maynard

Richard Rodger

**Software
Made
Simple**

Software Made Simple
R and G Design Ltd
Unit E, Troon Way Business Centre,
Humberstone Lane, Leicester LE4 7JW
Telephone 0116 2461424

Technical Information: Mark Maynard 0116 2522844

The Authors

Adrian Beck is a Lecturer in Security and Information Technology at
the Centre for the Study of Public Order, University of Leicester

Mark Maynard is a Senior Computing Officer at the University of Leicester

Richard Rodger is a Senior Lecturer in the Economic and Social History Department, University of Leicester

Other Guides in This Series

A Student's Guide to FileMaker Pro 2 for the Macintosh and the IBM PC Compatible

A Student's Guide to WordPerfect 5.2 for Windows for the IBM PC Compatible

A Student's Guide to FoxPro 2.5 for the Macintosh and the IBM PC Compatible

A Student's Guide to Excel 4 for the Macintosh and the IBM PC Compatible

A Student's Guide to Excel 5 for the Macintosh and the IBM PC Compatible

A Student's Guide to Word for Windows for the IBM PC Compatible

A Student's Guide to Cricket Graph for the Macintosh

A Student's Guide to Word 5 for the Macintosh

A Student's Guide to Word 4 for the Macintosh

For further information on these guides please contact:

Software Made Simple
R and G Design Ltd
Unit E, Troon Way Business Centre,
Humberstone Lane, Leicester LE4 7JW
Telephone 0116 2461424

Technical Information: Mark Maynard 0116 2522844

This guide is based on using a complete default installation of
Microsoft Word 6 for Windows on an IBM PC or compatible with a
hard disc and Windows 3.1 in standard mode using a mouse.
For printing, use of a network is also assumed.

For simplicity the term PC is used throughout to mean IBM PC compatible.

Version 1

ISBN 1 874093 10 5

CONTENTS

SECTION 1 GETTING STARTED ON THE PC

SECTION 2 GETTING STARTED WITH WORD FOR WINDOWS

SECTION 3   MORE ADVANCED WORDPROCESSING

QUICK START

If you are familiar with Windows move on to Section 2.

If you are in a hurry but are unfamiliar with the PC, Windows or the mouse you should at least read Sections 1.1 to 1.12 *(up to the File Manager)* and then move on to Section 2. However, be aware that Section 2 assumes that you will have read and understood all of Section 1.

S E C T I O N 1

Getting Started on the PC

1.1

Introduction

This guide aims to introduce you to the PC computer and Windows, and to show you how to use the popular Wordprocessor, Microsoft Word for Windows. The guide was written mostly with students in mind so it emphasises their special requirements like generating footnotes, tables and title pages.

The principles outlined in this guide are simple and intuitive, so even if you've never used a computer before, don't be intimidated. This guide assumes no previous experience of computers, although a basic understanding of the common elements of the keyboard is assumed.

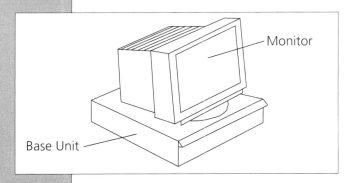

The PC comes equipped with a monitor (screen), a base unit (the box housing the computer and hard disc usually situated under or alongside the monitor), a keyboard and a mouse (a plastic cube with a wire coming out of it and two buttons on top). All of these components will become familiar to you as you read through the guide.

When you switch on a PC, the computer starts up a computer program known as an Operating System, which allows you to manipulate information or files. On the PC this Operating System is known as DOS. However, DOS can be intimidating to use and an alternative form of manipulating files has been developed that works alongside DOS. This is known as Windows. You need to know a little about how to use Windows before you can use the wordprocessor, Word for Windows.

1.2

Turning on the PC

To turn on the PC switch on the Monitor (screen), press a button at the bottom of the monitor, or by flicking a switch on the side. Also, switch on the Base unit, by flicking up a switch normally on the right hand side of the base unit. The computer will now start, and will take about a minute.

Problem? The screen has been completely blank for over a minute.

Solution: Either, the brightness of the screen is turned down in which case turn the brightness knob normally located underneath the screen, or the electricity isn't getting to the computer. Are both the monitor and the base unit switched on? Are they switched on at the plug? Seek assistance if you still get problems.

Problem? For over a minute a number has been displayed in the top left hand corner of the screen.

Solution: There is a fault with the computer. Seek assistance.

Problem? A small line is shown on the top left hand corner of the screen and a chugging noise is heard.

Solution: There is a floppy disc in the floppy disc drive. Eject the floppy disc by pressing the button alongside the drive and switch the computer off and on again.

Starting up Windows

Before you can use Word for Windows you must first start Windows. How you do this depends on how the computer has been configured.

- If you see this on the screen:

        C:\>

This is called a C prompt and indicates that you are now using DOS (see Section 1.1). To start up Windows you need to type in the command **Win** and press the **Enter** (↵) key.

- If you see this on the screen:

        F:\LOGIN>

then the computer you are using requires you to have a Username and Password. If you do not have a Username and Password or are unsure how to use the one you have, seek assistance. Once you have entered your Username and Password you will probably be presented with a number of choices as below. If not, seek assistance.

- Your computer may be configured to start up Windows automatically.

- You may have to select from a number of choices presented to you on the screen, one of which will be Windows. Generally to select a choice use the Arrow keys on the keyboard and press the **Enter** (↵) key.

The Desktop

Which ever way your computer is configured the screen display should now be similar to the figure opposite.

This is called the **Desktop**. If your screen doesn't look exactly like this, don't worry; someone else has probably arranged it differently. After you learn to use the **Mouse** you will be able to handle the desktop and arrange the items displayed in the way that you want.

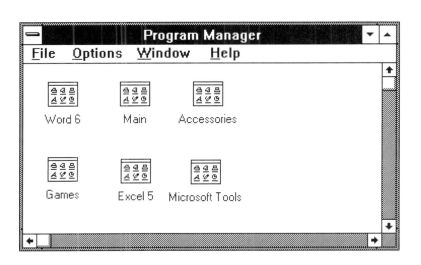

Using the Mouse

Using the Mouse is central to the way Windows works and you will find that you can do most things you want to do with windows just by using the mouse.

You will notice a black outlined white arrow somewhere on the screen; this is known as the Mouse pointer or Pointer. Every move you make with the mouse resting on the desk moves the pointer in exactly the same way. Usually the pointer is shaped like an arrow, as above, but it changes shape depending on what you are doing.

For instance, it becomes:

I, an 'I-beam', when it is positioned over text you can edit,

$|$, a flashing 'beam', at the current insertion point,

$\boxtimes$, an hour glass, when the computer is performing a task that takes a little time.

You will have best control over the pointer if you hold the mouse with the mouse cable pointing directly away from you. If you run out of room for the mouse, if it goes off the table, for instance, lift the mouse up and put it down again where you have more room. Lifting the mouse does not move the pointer. Using the mouse might feel a little awkward at first, but it will soon be second nature to you. Like most things it needs a bit of practice.

There are two buttons on the top of the mouse, though only the left hand button need concern us. This button is used to select items on the screen.

Icons

Even if your desktop is arranged differently from the one illustrated above you will probably see one or more small pictures with names underneath. These small pictures, like those shown below, are known as Icons. Icons are intended to convey their meaning and function

Paintbrush   Notepad   Cardfile   Calculator

to the user and often they correspond to their purpose, eg the paint palette icon is a painting program.

Icons show you which Applications (computer programs) and documents are available.

APPLICATIONS	DOCUMENTS
These are Computer Programs or Software that you use on the computer to perform a particular type of task, for example:	These are created by Applications and may include:

APPLICATIONS:
- Wordprocessor for writing
- Spreadsheet for calculating
- Graphics for drawing

DOCUMENTS:
- Thesis written on a Wordprocessor
- Budget calculated on Spreadsheet
- Map drawn using a Graphics application

1.7

Paintbrush

Paintbrush

Selecting by Clicking

To do anything with an icon it must first be **Selected**. This is done by moving the pointer until its tip is on the icon you want to select, and clicking the mouse button once. To indicate that it is selected the name under the icon will be highlighted, as opposite.

Selecting is an important idea with Windows, and it has a specific meaning: you must always select the information if you want to adapt or amend it.

To change your mind, **De-select** the icon by clicking on something else.

1.8

Dragging

Once an icon has been selected you can use the mouse to move it with a technique called **Dragging**. This is useful if you want to re-arrange your desktop.

For example, position the pointer on any icon, then press and hold the mouse button down while you move the mouse. As you do this the pointer moves and drags the icon together with its name. And when you release the mouse button, the icon snaps into its new place.

Now select and drag the icon back to its original position. This technique is called **Click and Drag**.

1.9

Windows

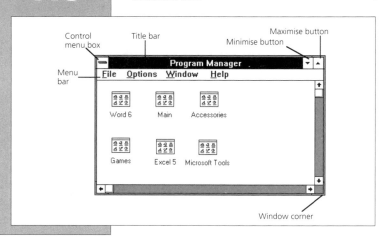

As mentioned above you may find that the desktop looks different to the one illustrated. One of the main differences will be the number and size of overlapping rectangles present. These rectangles are called Windows and they can be moved around, made bigger or smaller or removed.

Windows are used to show the contents of icons.

Each of the components of the window has a particular function and clicking on each component has a different effect:

Title Bar: where the name of the window is displayed, and by clicking and dragging, the entire window can be repositioned.

Window Corner: used to change the size of a window, click and drag this corner of the window to the required window size.

Control-Menu Box: clicked twice (double-clicked) to close the window.

Maximize Button: one click here makes the window as large as the screen will allow.

Minimize Button: one click here turns the window into an icon on the desktop.

Restore Button: visible only when a window has been maximized. One click will return the window to its previous size.

Menu Bar: see Section 1.11 below.

Scroll Bars: Because a window may contain many icons it is often impossible for them all to be displayed at once on the screen. Down the right-hand side and along the bottom of the window are **Scroll Bars** and **Scroll Arrows** which enable you move around the window to reveal other icons. By clicking on the scroll arrows you will notice that the scroll box moves and another part of the window is revealed to you. If the window has no scroll bars there are no such hidden icons.

Two other ways of scrolling are to click and drag the scroll box along the scroll bar or to click in the scroll bar itself. Try them out; you will soon get the hang of scrolling.

A window can be moved just as icons can. To move a window, position the pointer anywhere on the title bar and click and drag the window to its required position.

1.10 Using Windows

The important parts of Windows are the **Program Manager** and the **File Manager**. Both use the windows and the mouse described above so it is important to have grasped the techniques above before proceeding.

The **Program Manager** is used to start up applications like Word for Windows. It is most commonly used to start on a new document, eg. an essay.

The **File Manager** is used to manipulate and organise files, which includes applications and any documents or other files you create. With the File Manager you give them names and store them together as you wish. Though you can also start up applications with the File Manager it is not as straight-forward as using Program Manager.

1.11 The Program Manager

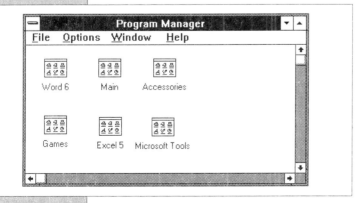

Before we look at the **Program Manager** it will help to reduce screen clutter. To do this **Minimise** (see above) all the open windows on your screen except the one entitled **Program Manager**.

The Program Manager is the part of Windows where you choose which application to use. It is where you start up Word for Windows to work on a new document. The **Program Manager** appears on the desktop as in the figure opposite.

Like all applications, the **Program Manager** has a **Menu Bar** below its title bar. This menu bar provides access to commands which operate the application. In the **Menu Bar**, are the titles of the different menus which you can choose.

Generally menu commands require you to have selected something before they are applied, eg. select an icon. This tells the computer what you want the command to take effect on. Next move the pointer to the name of one of the menus and click the mouse button. This will reveal the commands available under the particular menu, the exact appearance of which will depend upon the particular menu chosen, but you will see something like the **File** menu opposite.

The items listed under the menu are called **Commands**. A command can be chosen by moving the pointer down the list and clicking on the chosen command, this will cause the command to be carried out. Some commands in the list may be grey; this means that for the moment they cannot be chosen. Only those listed in black can be chosen.

The Icons shown in the Program Managers window are **Group icons**.

Group icons represent collections of applications of a particular type; Accessories, Games, or group icons containing particular Applications. Within each of these groups are icons which represent any applications installed on the computer's hard disc, like Word for Windows. The "*Main*" group icon is special; it controls some of the functions of windows.

To look at the contents of any Group icon it must first be opened. To do this:

- Select the Group icon by clicking on it.

- Position the tip of the pointer on the word **File** in the menu bar and click the mouse button. This causes the file menu to appear, as above.

- Move the pointer to the command **Open**, and click the mouse button once more.

The result is that a Window will open with the same name as the group icon. You will probably also notice that the Group icon has now disappeared from the desktop. The icons contained within the group icon are revealed in a window of their own (group window) which is opened within the Program Manager window (once opened any group window is constrained to within the boundary of the Program Manager window).

A shortcut to choosing the **Open** command from the **File** menu is to click the mouse button twice (**double-click**) on the icon in quick succession.

To open (start up) any of these applications just double-click on the appropriate icon. Using applications you create documents or files.

Managing Files

The **File Manager** is the part of Windows where you organise the files or documents created using the applications from the Program Manager. These are organised into disc drives and directories.

1.12

Disc Drives

Documents and applications can be stored in one of two places – on a **Hard Disc** or on a **Floppy Disc**. The hard disc drive is inside the base unit of the computer; the floppy disc drive is also in the base unit but the floppy discs it uses are removable.

Each kind of disc drive has its own advantages and disadvantages:

	ADVANTAGES	DISADVANTAGES
HARD DISC	Fast Large capacity	Expensive Not portable Not yours
FLOPPY DISC	Portable Yours Cheap	Slow Smaller capacity

The Hard disc has the advantage that it has much more room on it to store information, even the smallest hard disc can store about 20,000k (Kilobytes) or 20Mb (Megabytes) of information, equivalent to about 20 million letters or 4 million words, whereas a floppy disc can only store about 700k (Kilobytes) of information, equivalent to about 700,000 letters or 140,000 words.

Floppy disc drives are labelled **A:** (and **B:** if there is more than one). Hard discs and Network disc drives are labelled **C:** to **Z:**.

Floppy discs need to be formatted before they can be used (see Section 1.22).

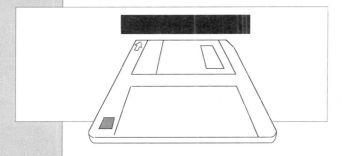

To use the floppy disc drive you need to insert a floppy disc into the slot in the base unit of the computer. The floppy disc **MUST** be put in with the metal rectangle towards the computer and the metal circle facing **DOWNWARDS**. Unlike some floppy discs you can't turn this type over.

To remove (eject) a floppy disc press the button near the disc drive.

Types of Floppy Discs

There are two types of floppy disc that concern us. Both look very similar but one has an additional square hole as marked HD as shown in the example below.

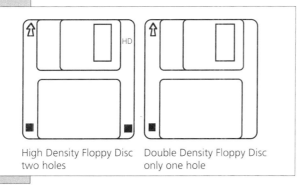

High Density Floppy Disc
two holes

Double Density Floppy Disc
only one hole

The type with the two holes is a HIGH DENSITY disc and should be used only with certain IBM PC compatibles; sometimes these display 1.44 on the eject button nearby the floppy disc drive slot.

The type with the one hole is a DOUBLE DENSITY disc and can be used with any IBM PC compatible.

1.13

The advantage of using High Density floppy discs is that they are capable of storing around twice as much information (1.44Mb) as Double Density floppy discs (0.7Mb).

Using the File Manager

To start the **File Manager** first open the **Main** group icon from the Program Manager by double-clicking. Then open the File Manager icon from the window that appears. The result will be similar to the Directory window figure shown below.

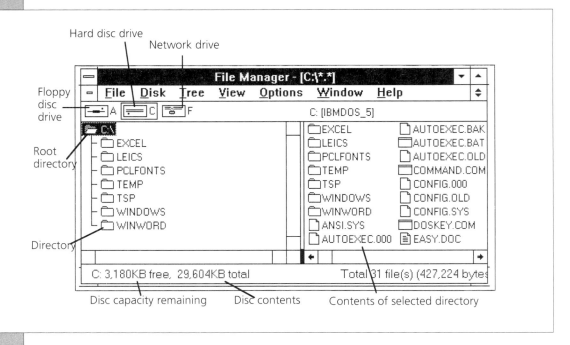

Hard disc drive

Network drive

Floppy disc drive

Root directory

Directory

Disc capacity remaining   Disc contents   Contents of selected directory

The Directory window shows the presence of floppy disc drives, hard disc drives and network disc drives; each is labelled with a letter. By selecting one of the drives its contents are displayed.

Files on either floppy or hard discs are organised into **Directories**. You can put files which are related into directories, and naming the directory with a title which describes its contents helps you to organise your work. For example, if you have several files concerning Leicestershire it would be sensible to put all these files into a directory called *"Leics"*. You could also make a sub-directory within the directory *"Leics"* called *"Rutland"* into which you would put all your files concerning Rutland. This would form a tree structure, see below.

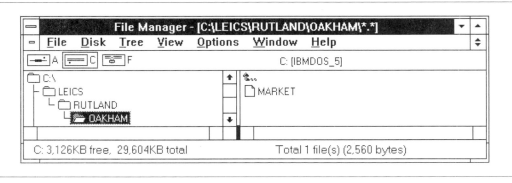

This sort of tree is represented on the left side of the directory window. However, only directories and sub-directories are displayed, and these are represented with a particular icon.

From the left half of the window directories are selected, and in the right hand half of the window the contents of the selected directory and of any sub-directories, are displayed.

On the right side of the directory window other File Manager icons are also displayed. These consist of program files (applications), document files or other files. Each is represented by a different icon.

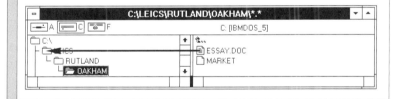

Alongside each icon is a file name. Normally this consists of the name of the file and an extension (suffix), eg. ESSAY.DOC. The extension informs you about the type of file it is. Here '.**DOC**' indicates a Word for Windows file. The extension '.**EXE**' tells you that the file is an application.

You have seen that applications can be opened (started up) from the **Program Manager** by double-clicking on the application icon, but you can also open them by double-clicking the appropriate icon within File Manager. Perhaps more useful is if you double-click on a document file icon since it will open both the document and the application that created it.

Creating a New Directory

From the left side of the directory window you must choose the directory in which you want the directory to be created. Choose the **Create Directory** command from the **File** menu. A dialogue box is displayed which asks you to type in a name for the directory. Do this, and then click on the **OK** button. A new directory will appear in the directory window.

Moving Icons into a Directory or Disc

So as to organise your files sensibly you should move their icons into an appropriately named directory. To do this you must be able to see in the directory window both the icon of the file that you want to move and the icon of the directory where you want to move it.

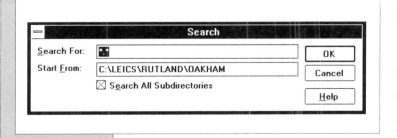

To move an icon into another directory click and drag it from its current directory window to the icon or window of the destination directory. You will be asked whether you are sure that you want to move the file. Click on **Yes**; the icon will be moved, and will have disappeared from its original location.

The same method can be used to copy an icon from one disc to another by clicking and dragging the icon to the disc icons displayed at the top of the File Manager window.

Searching For a File

It is very easy to forget exactly in which directory you put a particular file. To save searching through all your directories there is a short cut if you can remember the name of the file. Click on the disc drive where you know the file to be and choose the **Search** command from the **File** menu. A dialogue box like the one opposite will be displayed. Type in the name of the file and its extension. Another dialogue box will appear showing you the results of the search. You can double-click on the file in the dialogue box to open it directly.

Naming Files and Directories

Names of files and directories can be changed quite easily by clicking once on their icon and choosing the **Rename** command from the **File** menu. A dialogue box is presented which gives the current name of the file or directory; to rename it type in the box provided and click on **OK**.

IMPORTANT: File and directory names in windows can only be 8 letters or numbers (characters) long, excluding any extension. Also they cannot contain any spaces or the following characters, /.[];="`:l,.

Removing Files, Applications and Directories

To remove a file, application or directory all you need to do is select its icon and choose the **Delete** command from the **File** menu. A dialogue box is presented asking you to confirm the deletion. If you are deleting a directory with files inside, another dialogue box is presented. You can choose to delete all the files in the directory by clicking on **Yes to all**. **Click** on **OK** if you are sure.

Exiting File Manager

To exit File Manager choose the **Exit** command from the **File** menu. You will be asked to confirm your decision.

Exiting Program Manager and Windows

You cannot exit Program Manager without exiting Windows itself. Choose the command **Exit Windows** from the Program Manager **File** menu or double-click on the **Control menu box**.

You will now be returned to the display that you first saw when you turned on the computer. If you are attached to a network you must type **Logoff** or choose the **Logoff** command from the menu provided.

Turning Off

It is important to follow the correct steps to switch off otherwise you can damage the computer.

If you are using an application, choose **Exit** from the **File** menu, saving work as required. Exit from Windows, see Section 1.20.

Switch off the computer both at the button on the monitor and on the base unit. See Section 1.2.

1.22 How to Format a Floppy Disc

Generally when floppy discs are bought they need to be **Formatted** (Initialised) before they can be used. Formatting marks out areas on the disc where information is to be stored and makes a record of where the storage areas are so that information can be retrieved quickly.

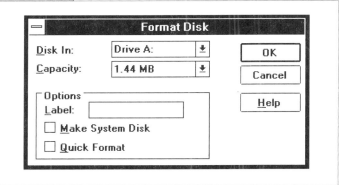

To Format a disc, start up **File Manager** and put the floppy disc into the disc drive. Click on the icon of the floppy disc drive and a dialogue box will be displayed asking if you wish to format the disc. Click on **Yes**. Another dialogue box will be presented showing an estimate of the capacity of your floppy disc. It is very important that for double density discs this figure is set to 720k and for high density discs 1.44 Mb. If you are unsure, see Section 1.12 on types of floppy disc. Click on **OK**.

You will be asked to confirm your decision as formatting deletes all information from the disc. If you click on **Format** another dialogue box like the one above will be presented. Just click on **OK**.

Formatting will take about a minute and a dialogue box showing its progress will be displayed. When complete the disc is ready for use.

Note: Do not assume that the default capacity is correct. If you do and it is incorrect you may have problems using the disc on other computers.

1.23 Making Floppy Disc Backups

Although putting information on a floppy disc is reasonably secure, occasionally things go wrong and information is lost. To reduce the chance of any such loss you should keep an identical copy on a different floppy disc and store it in a different place. This is called making a backup. There are a number of ways to do this backup but the easiest is as follows.

For this you will need a disc for backup and blank formatted floppy disc.

IMPORTANT: You must make sure that the capacity of the floppy disc you are copying to is the same or greater than the capacity of the floppy disc you are copying from. See Section 1.12 on Types of Floppy Disc.

- Write protect the disc that you wish to backup (see below).

- Open the File Manager.

- Choose the **Copy Disk** command from the **Disk** menu. A warning dialogue box will be displayed click on **Yes**.

- Insert the floppy disc for backup (source) into the drive when prompted.

- Insert the blank formatted floppy disc into the drive when prompted.

Locking or Write-protecting Floppy Discs

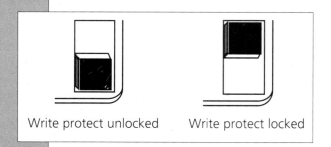

Write protect unlocked   Write protect locked

Once you have made a backup it is a good idea to lock or **write-protect** it to prevent accidental erasure. To lock a floppy disc eject it from the computer and turn it over. In the right hand corner you will see a little square hole with a switch.

To lock the disc move the switch to open the hole. The reverse unlocks the disc and removes the write protection.

Help

For reasons of space, this guide only provides the basics of how to get started using Windows and Word for Windows. For more detail, see the relevant **Microsoft User's Guide**.

Assistance with Windows is also provided by using the **Search for Help On** command from the **Help** menu and the on-line **Windows tutorial** also from the **Help** menu.

For assistance with Word see Section 2.29.

1.24

S E C T I O N 2

Getting Started With Word for Windows

2.1

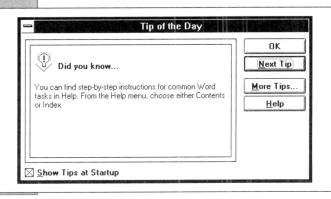

Starting Word for Windows

Using the **Program Manager** find the icon for **Word for Windows**.

The icon will probably be titled **Microsoft Word** and in a group called **Word for Windows, Word 6** or **Winword**. Double-click on the icon. An hour glass will replace the normal arrow pointer while Word for Windows starts up and transfers into the computer's memory from the hard disc. A screen will appear similar to the illustration below

This guide assumes that the Ruler and Formatting Toolbar are shown on screen. If any of these is not shown, choose the appropriate command from the **View** menu. Also ensure that the view is set to **Normal** by checking that a • is shown alongside **Normal** in the **View** menu.

2.2

Tip of the Day

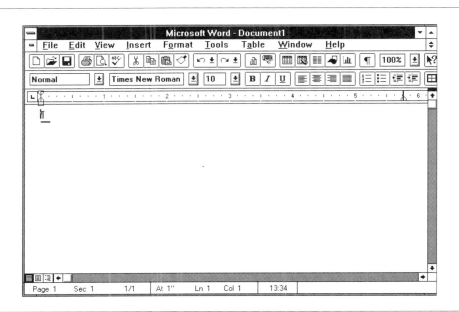

By default Word will probably display a tip of the day.

This is intended to provide suggestions to help you learn to use Word more effectively. If you wish to stop Tip of the Day being displayed click in the **Show Tips at Startup** box.

2.3

Creating a New File

When you start up Word a blank document window titled **Document1** will be displayed on the screen. Should you need to open a new document, choose the **New** command from the **File** menu or click on the ☐ button on the Toolbar and click on the **OK** button of the dialogue box presented.

2.4

Typing in Text

You should see that there are two marks in the document window even before you start to type; a ¶ mark and a horizontal line. If you do not see these marks click on the ☐ button on the Toolbar. These marks already on screen do not print and are there merely as a guide.

The ¶ mark indicates the end of a paragraph and appears when you press the **Enter** (↵) key. The space between two ¶ marks is defined by Word as a **Paragraph** (so a paragraph defined by Word can be a space, a word, a sentence etc. anything as long as it begins and ends with one of these ¶ markers).

The horizontal line indicates the end of your document.

If you don't like these markers or the small non-printing dot which appears each time you use the space bar, they can be hidden by clicking on the ☐ button on the Toolbar. However, they are very useful for editing purposes.

Text which you type will appear to the left of the blinking vertical line on the screen. This line is called the **Insertion point**. The insertion point can be moved around the screen in one of two ways:

- By using the mouse to move the **Pointer**, click the mouse button where you want to move the insertion point. Note: the pointer changes shape to I when on top of text.

- By pressing the **Arrow** keys to move one space at a time or holding the **Arrow** key down to move more than one space at a time.

Note the distinction between the **Pointer** and the **Insertion point**: the insertion point is always a blinking vertical line whilst the Pointer is moved around by the mouse and changes its appearance according to its position on the screen.

As you type in text, it is **NOT** necessary to press the **Enter** (↵) key at the end of each line as you do with a typewriter. With a wordprocessor you just keep on typing and the words will flow automatically on to the next line for you. It is only necessary to press the **Enter** key if you want to start a new paragraph, and then you should only press it **ONCE**.

If you make a mistake typing in your text just move the insertion point to the right of the mistake and press the **Backspace** (←) key. You can delete the ¶ paragraph markers in the same way.

Text can be inserted by moving the insertion point to the appropriate place and then typing.

The wordprocessor will tell you when you have typed more text than will fit onto an A4 page by putting a non-printing dotted line across the screen. The dotted line forms the start of a new page. The bottom left hand corner of the window displays the number of the page on which you are working.

2.5 Selecting Text

To select a word or character, move the insertion point to the left of the text you wish to select, click and hold down the mouse button, and move the mouse to the right. As you move the mouse the selected word or character will be inverted as in **White Characters**. This technique is called click and drag.

To select several words follow the click and drag method above only releasing the mouse button when all the required words are selected. Note that this selection need not be all on one line; you can select across lines, across paragraphs or even the whole document in this way. You can select from right to left if you prefer. A quicker way to select the whole document is to use the **Select All** command from the **Edit** menu.

Problem? You try and select text but the text moves instead.

Solution: You have found a feature of word called **Drag and Drop** (see Section 2.19 for more information). To move the text back to its original position click on the **Undo** button on the Toolbar (see Section 2.14 for more information about Undo).

2.6 Scrolling

Normally the screen is a **Window** or partial view of your document. To see other parts of the document you can:

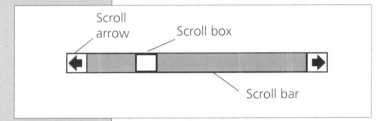

Scroll arrow

Scroll box

Scroll bar

- Click on the scroll arrows to view the document line by line.

- Click on the grey area on the right-hand side of the scroll bar to move up and down the document a screen-full at a time.

- Click on the scroll box and drag it up or down to move between pages.

2.7 The Ruler and Formatting Toolbar

Two features of Word that are closely linked are the **Ruler** and **Formatting Toolbar**. These provide quick access to some of the most commonly used text formats you are likely to need.

Most of the problems that people encounter while using Word are due to lack of understanding of the Ruler and Formatting Toolbar and how they operate. So competent use of the these is one of the most important skills that you must master in order to be able to get the best from Word.

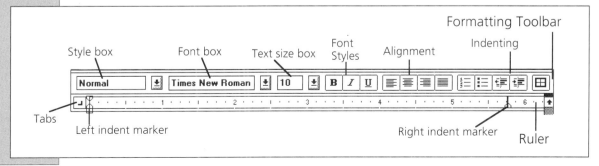

Formatting Toolbar

Style box · Font box · Text size box · Font Styles · Alignment · Indenting · Tabs · Left indent marker · Right indent marker · Ruler

Note: As the pointer moves over the buttons on the toolbar a pop-up box displays the function of the button.

The reason that the Ruler and Formatting Toolbar are so important is that they let you change the layout of your text. Using them you can:

- Set the distance from the left hand margin at which your text will begin.

- Set the distance from the right hand margin at which your text will end.

- Set the alignment of text to be left, right, centre or justified.

- Indent a paragraph.

- Change the Font, Character style and Size of text.

It is best if you set the layout of your text using the Ruler and Formatting Toolbar before you begin to type because from then all your typing will have this layout. However, if you prefer you can change the layout after typing in the text.

It is very important to note that for any of these changes to the Ruler to have any effect on text already typed in you must either:

Select all the text you want to change.

Or, if you only want to change the layout of one paragraph, make sure the insertion point is in that paragraph.

2.8 Aligning Paragraphs

The four buttons on the right of the Toolbar are used for alignment. These allow you to align text in which ever way you prefer just by clicking on the button.

Aligns the text to the **left** margin – the normal setting.

Aligns text **centrally** – useful for headings.

Aligns text to the **right** – useful for addresses in letters.

justifies text. This means both **left** and **right** sides of the text are aligned with the margins – like a book or a newspaper.

2.9 Indenting Paragraphs

The **Indent markers** on the left and right of the Ruler can be clicked and dragged along the Ruler to increase or decrease the margin width for the **selected** text. This is called indenting.

Be sure to click and drag only the lower of the two triangles of the Indent marker on the left unless you want the special indenting described below.

The Indent mark on the left is different from that on the right as it can be split into two. The reason for this is that the upper half of the marker represents the first line of the paragraph whilst the lower half represents the remainder. This is useful as you often want the first line of a paragraph to be laid out differently from the rest of the paragraph.

HINT: A Quick way of indenting is to use the button on the Toolbar which will indent the selected text by a predetermined distance to the default 0.5 in (1.27cm). Click on the button to remove the indent.

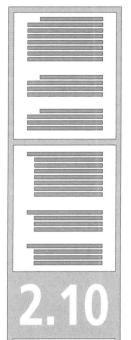

Indenting the First Line of Paragraphs

Assuming you want to indent paragraphs that you have already typed in, select the paragraphs, and click and drag the top of the left indent mark to the place on the Ruler where you want your first line to be indented. This will indent the first line of every paragraph selected. If you haven't yet typed in your paragraph just move the indent marker as above and start typing.

Indenting the Whole Paragraph Except the First Line

This kind of indent is called a **Hanging indent** and can be very effective in presentation. If you haven't yet typed in your paragraph just move the indent marker as above and start typing. Otherwise, with text already typed, a hanging indent is obtained by selecting the paragraph(s), and while holding the shift (⇧) key, clicking and dragging on the ruler where you want the indent to be. This will indent all but the first line of every selected paragraph.

Changing Size, Font and Character Style of Text

One of the clever things about wordprocessing with Word is that every word, letter and line can be written in a different font, character style or size.

You can either set the font, character style or size before you start typing or once you have typed it in. For text already typed you must first select the characters, lines or paragraphs you want to change before following the instructions below.

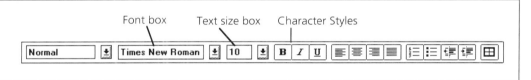

The current size of the text is displayed in the text size box on the Toolbar. To change this size, click on the arrow and choose the required size as you would a command from the menu bar, or type a size into the box. Sizes are measured in points or pts, 10 or 12 pts is normal, the bigger the point size the bigger the text. For other sizes of text outside this range see Section 3.7.

For different font styles use the buttons on the Toolbar:

B produces **bold** text.

I produces *italic* text.

U produces Underlined text.

To de-select any of these character styles simply select the text and click on the particular character style button again. Other character styles are available by choosing the **Character** command from the **Format** menu.

Another way of changing the appearance of your text is to change its **Font** (Typeface). As you will see by clicking on the arrow to the right of the font name box on the Toolbar, fonts are given all sorts of peculiar names. Select one of these fonts as you would a command from the menu bar.

2.11 Changing the Spacing Between Lines and Paragraphs

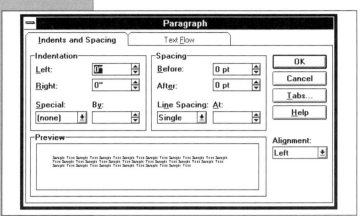

The default spacing between all lines of text is single line spacing. However, using single line spacing can make your text appear cramped. The line spacing can be set individually for each paragraph or for the whole document. To change the line spacing select your text and choose the **Paragraph** command from the **Format** menu. A dialogue box will be presented.

The current line spacing is displayed in a box under the heading line spacing. The line spacing can be set to Single, 1.5, or Double by clicking and dragging on the arrow alongside.

The **before** and **after** options in the paragraph dialogue box allow you to set the amount of space above or below each paragraph. Select a different paragraph spacing by clicking on the arrow buttons alongside each box.

The effect that changing the line and paragraph spacing will have on the text can be seen in the previewed sample box in the bottom right corner of the dialogue box. Click on **OK** to have the spacing change take effect.

2.12 Copying a Format

Once a piece of text has been formatted you can copy its formatting onto another piece of text by using the **Painter** tool.

- Select the text containing the formatting you wish to copy and choose the ⌖ button from the Toolbar.

- Select the text you wish to copy the format to, release the mouse button, and the format is copied.

2.13 Page Breaks

Word automatically puts in page breaks when you type more text than can fit on an A4 page. However, often you will want to start a new page before your text reaches the bottom of a page. To do this, choose the **Break** command from the **Insert** menu. A dialogue box will appear; just click on **OK**.

A fine dotted line will appear across the page indicating the presence of a user inserted page break. The user inserted page break line can be easily distinguished from the automatic one as it is made up of more dots.

```
..................................................................................   ———— Automatic page break

.......................Page Break.......................   ———— User inserted page break
```

Unlike automatically inserted page breaks, a page break which you have inserted deliberately can be deleted. To do this, move the insertion point to before the first character after the page break and press the **Backspace** (←) key.

2.14 Undo Command

One useful facility that you will soon grow to love is **Undo**. This is available by clicking on the ⟨↰ ⟩ button on the Toolbar.

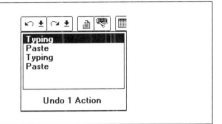

The last changes which you made to your document are listed below the button and any one can be undone by choosing the item on the list.

Conversely, using the **Redo** button ⟨↱ ⟩ on the Toolbar reverses any changes you have made using the undo button.

2.15 Saving Your Work

When you decide that you want to stop wordprocessing you should save your work so that you can finish it off another day. To save a new piece of work, choose **Save As** from the **File** menu. A dialogue box appears like the one below.

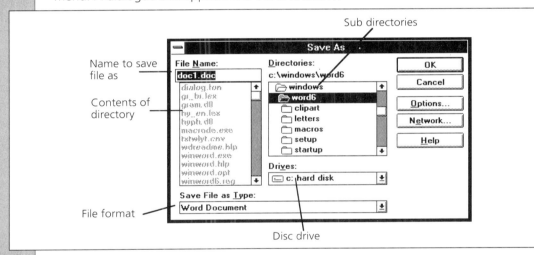

First choose where to save your work from the drives list by clicking on the arrow alongside the drives box. Next click on the file name box and type a file name for your document. An extension '**.DOC**' will automatically be added to the file name so that it can be distinguished as a Word file.

It may be necessary to scroll up the list if you wish to save on a floppy disc. The floppy disc drive is drive **a:** or **b:** and the hard disc usually drive **c:**. If you have a network other drives may be available.

IMPORTANT: File and directory names in windows can only be 8 letters or numbers (characters) long, excluding any extension. Also they cannot contain any spaces or the following characters, /.[];=""`:l,.

Problem? You cannot select the drive to which you want to save.

Solution: Insert your floppy disc into the disc drive, and ensure that the floppy disc is formatted. See Section 1.22.

Problem? You've got a message saying "This is not a valid file name".

Solution: See the above notes on file name restrictions.

To save your work either click on the **OK** button or press the **Enter** (↵) key. The file has now been saved and is safe until you or somebody else decides to delete it. Of course, if you save on your own floppy disc then you retain control.

> **Problem?** You are presented with the message "Word cannot create or save this file".
>
> **Solution:** Your disc is probably write protected, see Section 1.23.

If you share the computer avoid saving anything to Drive C: (the hard disc), as it may be deleted or altered by others who share access to the computer.

If the disc already has directories saved on to it you can see them by double-clicking on the drive letter. Sub-directories can also be viewed by double-clicking on the name of the directory in which they appear. This way you can choose to save a file directly into a specific directory. You may need to scroll through the directories to identify the particular one in which you want to save your work.

A titled file (one that has already been saved previously), can be updated and replaced by using the **Save** command from the **File** menu or by clicking on the save button 🖫 on the Toolbar.

By default every 10 minutes Word automatically saves your document for you as a temporary file. This can be useful in the event of a power failure as when you restart Word you will be prompted to recover the document. However, this feature should not be relied upon and the **Save** command should be used routinely every 10 minutes or so.

> Note: You may wish to switch off the automatic saving feature of Word as saving takes time and can interrupt the flow of your typing. To do this choose **Options** from the **Tools** menu and from the dialogue box presented click on the **Save** tab. To turn off automatic saving click on the box alongside **Automatically save every X minutes** and click on **OK**. However, remember to save manually at regular intervals.

2.16 Printing Your Work

You may have noticed an option under the **File** menu called **Print DON'T** use this just yet. First you must decide which printer you are going to use. Choose the command **Page Setup** from the **File** menu. This presents a dialogue box like the one below.

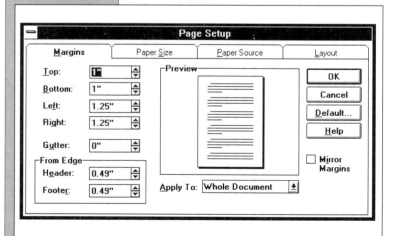

Along the top of the dialogue box are a series of **Tabs**. Clicking on one of these tabs displays options relating to the tab title. Click on the **Paper Size** tab and check that the paper set up is for A4 and that the orientation is correct. When you are satisfied click on the **OK** button.

Next, choose **Print Preview** from the **File** menu. This provides you with a *bird's eye view* of the page and is very useful for checking page breaks. Use the scroll bar at the side to move through the pages of your work. Click on the **Close** button when you have finished checking.

Lastly, choose **Print** from the **File** menu. The following dialogue box is presented.

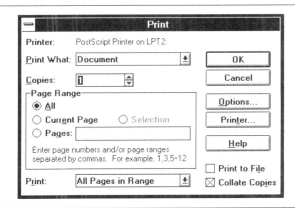

Choose the printer you wish to use by clicking on the **Printer** button. This displays the following dialogue box.

Make your selection from the printers available (if it is unclear from the printer names listed which is the most appropriate, seek assistance).

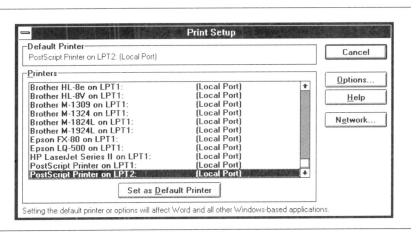

Hint: Before you print on a dot-matrix printer it is a good idea to check that the paper is wound to the right place in the printer. The perforation should be just above the roller; if it is not, turn the knob until it is.

In the print dialogue box you can choose to print all the document, the currently displayed page, or a specific range of pages. To print a range of pages click on the **Pages** button and enter the first and last page numbers separated by a hyphen eg. 3 - 5. To print all pages up to a particular page type the page number preceded by a hyphen. To print all pages after a particular page type the page number followed by a hyphen. To print a single page just type the page number.

Click on the **OK** button and your text will be printed. How long it will take to print depends how many other people are also printing and the complexity and length of your text. If you have waited more than 15 minutes, seek assistance.

Hint: As a short cut to printing, if you have chosen the printer set up you wish to use just click on the ⎙ button on the Toolbar.

Problem?: You are presented with a warning dialogue box telling you that the printer is out of paper or not connected.

Solution: Seek assistance.

2.17

To Exit From Your Document

To stop working on your document choose **Close** from the **File** menu. If you have not saved or have made any changes to the text you were working on you will be asked if you want to save your work.

Yes saves all changes before closing or exiting; **No** closes the file without saving any changes since the last **Save**. The **cancel** button cancels the **Close** or **Exit** command.

To stop using Word altogether simply choose **Exit** from the **File** menu. To exit Windows follow the instructions in Section 1.20.

To turn off the computer it is important that you follow the instructions in Section 1.21.

2.18

Opening an Existing File

To open a file that has already been saved choose **Open** from the **File** menu or click on the button on the Toolbar. A dialogue box appears (similar to the Save dialogue box shown previously), and this lists all the files which can be opened by Word. To open a particular file select the disc drive and directory where the file is located, and when the desired file name appears on the left of the dialogue box, open it in one of two ways: either by clicking on the file name and then on the **OK** button, or by double-clicking the file name.

Word allows you to open more than one file at a time and the various windows will be placed one on top of the other like a pile of papers on a desktop. To change from one to the other use the **Window** menu to select the file on which you want to work. To view all windows at once use the **Arrange All** command from the **Windows** menu. The current window can also be moved up or down or to one side by clicking and dragging on the title bar at the top of the window.

2.19

Moving Text Around a Document

When you are wordprocessing there are always times when you want to move or duplicate pieces of text. To avoid retyping, Word provides you with two techniques for doing this: **Drag and Drop**; and **Cut, Copy and Paste**.

Drag and Drop

Drag and Drop is most useful for moving small pieces of text for short distances about a document. For example you might wish to transpose two words.

* Select the text that you wish to move, and release the mouse button.

* Click and drag the text to its new position. You will notice a vertical line appears at the tip of the pointer; this is a guide to help you position the text precisely. If the new position of the text is currently not on screen, by moving the pointer to the top or bottom of the screen you can cause the text to scroll.

To copy a piece of text leaving the original intact hold down the **Ctrl** key while dragging.

Cutting, Copying and Pasting

These commands are most useful for moving or copying large pieces of text about a document.

To move a piece of text using Cut and Paste:

- Select the text to be moved.

- Choose **Cut** from the **Edit** menu or click on the ✂ button in the Toolbar. The text will disappear.

- Move the insertion point to where the text is to be placed.

- Choose **Paste** from the **Edit** Menu or click on the 📋 button in the Toolbar and the text will reappear to the right of the insertion point.

After the second step the text disappears from the screen. It is not lost but is stored on the **Clipboard**. This is a temporary storage area where anything cut or copied is stored. However, the clipboard can only store one item and so the next time you cut or copy what was previously on the clipboard is replaced by the newly cut or copied text.

To copy a piece of text:

Repeat the above procedure but choose **Copy** from the **Edit** Menu (click on the 📋 button on the Toolbar) instead of **Cut**. This will not make the selected text disappear but will put a copy of it on the clipboard.

Because the clipboard retains its contents after a **Paste** command it is possible to make several copies by simply using the **Paste** command as many times as is needed.

Tabs or Putting Text into Columns

On the left hand side of the ruler is the **Tab Alignment Button**. By clicking on this button you can change the type of tab stop. Each creates a column of text aligned in a different way. Keep clicking on the button until the tab stop you wish to use is displayed.

- ⌞ is a **Left tab** and aligns text to the left.

- ⊥ is a **Centre tab** and aligns text centrally either side of the tab.

- ⌟ is a **Right tab** and aligns text to the right.

- ⊥ is a **Decimal tab** and aligns numbers around the decimal point.

You can use as many of each tab stop as you want.

Click here

To use tab stops select the type you require, as above. Then click just below the Ruler at the point where you wish to position your column(s). The chosen tab stop will appear where you have clicked.

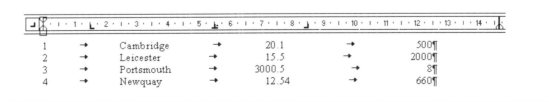

1	→	Cambridge	→	20.1	→	500¶
2	→	Leicester	→	15.5	→	2000¶
3	→	Portsmouth	→	3000.5	→	8¶
4	→	Newquay	→	12.54	→	660¶

Note: Ensure that you click in the space under the Ruler or tab stops will not appear.

2.20

If the first column is left aligned, as is most often the case (see above), then it is unnecessary to set a Tab for this column since normally it will be aligned with the left margin. The margin can be moved as required using the indent markers (Section 2.9).

To align text based on the tabs you have set up, type in the first item which will probably be aligned with the left margin. Now when you press the **TAB** (→|) key a non-printing arrow marker → appears and the insertion point is moved over to where you have set the first tab stop on the Ruler. Any text which you now type will appear at this point aligned according to the type of tab stop. Press the **TAB** (→|) key again and the insertion point will move to the next column, and so on. At the end of the row press the **Enter** (↵) key to return to the first column.

If you want to change any of the tab settings on the Ruler you must **select all** the text to which the tabs apply. You can then click and drag the tab stops to their new positions and the columns of text will follow.

Note: the Tab stops on the Ruler will disappear if you have selected text with different margins or tab set ups.

2.21 Presenting Lists of Information

Word provides two useful tools which allow you to quickly create bulleted (•) or numbered lists from paragraphs of text.

To use either of these tools:

* Each line that you wish to be bulleted or numbered must end with a paragraph marker (¶).

* Select the complete list.

* Click on the appropriate button on the Toolbar, 🔢 for a bulleted list, 🔢 for a numbered list.

Note: The style of bullet and the numbering scheme can be chosen by using the **Bullets and Numbering** command from the **Format** menu.

2.22 Borders

To draw attention to text or data, borders can be put around Paragraphs, Tables, Table Cells and Graphics using the same procedure.

First select the items around which you wish to put a border and click on the **Borders** button from the Toolbar. The **Borders** Toolbar is then displayed, either as a standard Toolbar or as a floating Toolbar which can be dragged about the screen by its title bar.

You can select the shading, line type, and thickness of the border from the Toolbar.

To remove the Toolbar from the screen choose **Toolbars** from the **View** menu, de-select the Toolbar, and click on **OK**.

2.23 Special Characters

The command **Symbol** from the **Insert** menu provides a dialogue box from which you can select symbols which are not readily available from the keyboard. For example: ê, á, Æ, Ö, Σ,©.

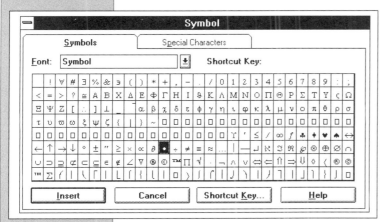

Each font has a number of characters that are not shown on the keyboard. To view these use the **Font** menu to choose the font that you wish to view. Select **Symbol** from the **Insert** menu. Clicking on any character in the dialogue box will cause the character to be inserted into your text at the insertion point.

Choose from the **Font** menu within the dialogue box to obtain alternative fonts and characters.

Using the **Symbol** command can be slow for entering commonly used international characters. An alternative is to use a combination of keys to create the character. Most combinations are intuitive for example, holding down **CTRL** and **'** while pressing **a** (**CTRL' & a**) displays à; **CTRL ^ & e** displays ê; **CTRL, & c** displays ç.

Fractions can be created using the **Equation Editor**, see Appendix D.

2.24 Spell Checking

Before you start to spell check save your work.

To check your spelling move the insertion point to the beginning of the text and choose **Spelling** from the **Tools** menu or click on the ⌨ button on the Toolbar. If the spell checker thinks a word is spelled incorrectly a dialogue box will be displayed.

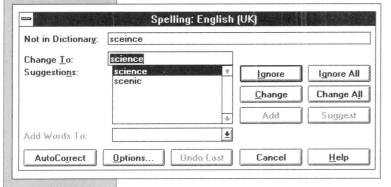

The dialogue box will list the word it thinks is spelled incorrectly. Often this word will not be mis-spelled, but just a word that the spell checker does not know – like your name for instance. If this is the case just click on the **Ignore** button. If the word is mis-spelled a list of alternatives will be presented. Select the correct spelling from these and click on the **Change** button to correct the spelling of the word in your text. Click on **Cancel** to stop spell checking.

If you are asked to continue spell checking from the beginning of the document this means that you forgot to move the insertion point to the start of the document. Unless you answer **Yes** you will have only spell checked your text from the insertion point to the end of the document and not the text before the insertion point.

HINT: Don't forget to save your work after you have spell checked it.

2.25 Word Count

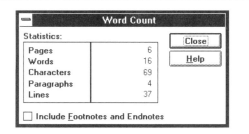

Word can count the number of words, characters, lines and paragraphs in your file so that you may check on how much you have (or haven't) typed. To display the word count choose **Word Count** from the **Tools** menu. When you've finished click on the **Cancel** button.

If you wish to count the number of words in a paragraph or piece of text first select it before choosing the **Word Count** command.

2.26 Finding and Replacing Text

If you want to find a word in a piece of text move the insertion point to the start of the text and use the **Find** command from the **Edit** menu, type in the word you want to find, and click on **OK**.

If you want to find and replace a word with another word throughout the document, use the **Replace** command from the **Edit** menu. Type in both the word that you want to search for and what you want to replace it with. Click on **Find Next** and on each occasion you will be asked whether you want the text replaced. Alternatively, click on **Replace All** to replace all occurrences of the text.

Beware: if, for example, you ask it to find all instances of the word **to** and replace them with **too**, words like **to**p and trai**to**r will be changed to **too**p and trai**too**r. To avoid this you can type spaces before or after the word to find or click on the **Match Whole Word Only** box.

2.27 AutoCorrect

Word's AutoCorrect feature prevents some of the most common typing errors, for example not capitalising the first word of a sentence, typing two capitals together eg. *WOrd*, automatically correcting common mis-types such as *teh* instead of *the*.

By default AutoCorrect is switched on so that these errors are corrected automatically as you type. Other common mis-types can be added to AutoCorrect by choosing **AutoCorrect** from the **Tools** menu and entering the error and the replacement in the boxes provided.

2.28 Short Cuts: The Alt and Ctrl Keys

You may find that using the mouse to choose commands from menus is a little awkward especially if you are a touch typist – if so, there is help at hand! You may have noticed that one letter of certain commands is underlined. For example the word above the **File** menu has the letter F underlined. This means that a short cut to using the mouse to pull down the **File** menu is while holding down the **Alt** key press the **F** key. Once a menu is pulled down you will notice more command short cuts like **Ctrl O** for **Open** and **Ctrl S** for **Save**.

2.29 Help with Word

Detailed **Help** using Word is available by clicking on the ⬚ button on the Toolbar this will turn the pointer into **?**. Clicking anywhere on screen will provide information on the object under the pointer. Most dialogue boxes also provide a **Help** button.

Assistance with Word is provided by using the **Help** menu. The **Quick Preview** command provides interactive lessons to get you started using Word. The **Search for Help on** command is useful to find help on a specific topic. The **Examples and Demos** command provides interactive help on a variety of common tasks.

Holding the mouse pointer on a button on the Toolbar displays the name of the button. For more detailed help refer to the **Microsoft Word Users' Guide**.

Good Habits for Typing in Text

So you've finished typing the text, checked the spelling, counted the words, admired your choice of fonts, and saved your text – but does is it look neat and presentable? Here are a number of pointers for getting that few extra marks for style:

- Type a single space after every comma and full stop.

- Don't put a space between the last letter of a word and any punctuation.

- Don't use <u>Underlining</u> unless you have to; there are far more elegant ways of emphasising text.

- Use a maximum of 2 or 3 fonts per document and don't mix together too many character styles eg. bold, italic etc. Take a look at the Five Pound note to see how ugly mixing too many fonts and character styles can look.

- Don't space paragraphs using the **Enter** (↵) key; set paragraph spacing using the **Paragraph** command.

- Don't cram text; use lots of spacing.

- Do define your styles; as shown in Section 3.

- Save your work as one complete document; avoid saving in parts, eg. chapters.

S E C T I O N   3

More Advanced Wordprocessing

3.1

Headers, Footers and Page Numbering

There are gaps left at the top and bottom of each page printed. These gaps are reserved for **Headers** and **Footers**. Headers and footers are pieces of text which appear on every printed page. You might wish a header to print the name of the chapter you are writing or a footer to print the page number at the bottom of each page.

A quick and easy way of adding basic page numbers to a document is to use the **Page numbers** command from the **Insert** menu. From the dialogue box presented you can select where the page numbers appear in the footer or header; you can also set the alignment. Click in the **Show Number on First Page** box to leave the first page un-numbered.

If you wish to add anything more than just a simple page number, the header or footer must be opened. To do this choose **Header and Footer** from the **View** menu. The view changes to **Page Layout** view (see Section 3.2) and the position of the header and footer are outlined on the page. Also displayed is the **Header and Footer Toolbar**.

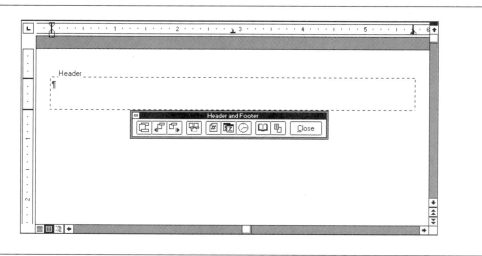

Use the button on the Toolbar to switch between the header and footer.

Move the insertion point to the header or footer and type in any text which you wish to appear on every page. The text can be aligned using the alignment buttons on the Toolbar just as for any other text, and doing this will not alter the alignment of your main text.

To make the date time or page number appear in the header or footer, click on the appropriate icon on the Toolbar. The page number will update for every page of the text. You can accompany this with other text if you wish, for example you might want to type '*Page*' before the page number. Once you have set up your headers and footers, click on the close button on the Toolbar.

Note: Do not type the page number into the footer, use the icons as described above.

Special Page Numbering

Setting up a page number in the manner described above will start page numbering at 1 and by default include numbering the first page. However, the title page of a document and the table of contents are not normally numbered, and other preliminary pages and acknowledgements are usually numbered differently from the main part of the document.

To start numbering a document from any number other than 1, insert the page number as above and choose the **Page Numbers** command from the **Insert** menu. From the dialogue box presented click on the **Format** button and from the following dialogue box enter the required page number in the **Start At** box.

To omit a page number from the first page and to have the second page numbered as 1 it is necessary to divide the document into two sections making the first page a different section. See Section 3.6 for information about Sections.

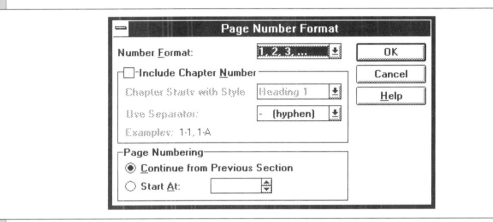

- Move the insertion point to the bottom of the first page and insert a section break as described in Section 3.6.

- Assuming that you have not already numbered the pages of the document, ensure the insertion point is in the second section and choose the **Page Numbers** command from the **Insert** menu. From the dialogue box presented click on the **Format** button and from the following dialogue box enter the page number you wish the second section to commence with in the **Start At** box.

- Move the insertion point back to the first page and delete any page breaks that you have inserted. Take care not to delete the section break. See Page Breaks Section 2.10.

- Use the **Print Preview** command to check that the page numbers are as required.

If you wish, you can make more than just the first page into a section, including things such as a contents page and acknowledgements. You can use as many sections as you like, perhaps creating a new section for each chapter.

You can also choose to number each section using a different number format, roman numerals are often used for preliminary pages preceding the main text. To do this insert the page number as above but from the **Page Numbers** dialogue box, click on the **Format** button. From the dialogue box presented click on the arrow alongside **Number format**.

To alter the information in the header or footer choose **Header and Footer** from the **View** menu and edit as normal. The **Backspace** (←) key can be used to delete markers inserted using the Toolbar eg. page numbers. Deleting information from the header or footer of one section will not affect the headers or footers of other sections.

3.2

Views

The standard view in Word is called the **Normal View** and this gives you an uncluttered view of your document by not showing things like headers, footers, footnotes etc.

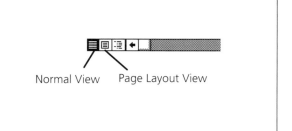

Normal View   Page Layout View

To see the page as it will be printed choose **Page Layout** from the **View** menu. However, **Page Layout** does not give a *bird's eye view* of the document; for this choose **Print Preview** from the **Edit** menu.

As an alternative to the menus the horizontal scroll bar at the bottom of the screen provides buttons which perform the same function.

The ▣ button on the Toolbar can be used instead of the Print Preview command.

The zoom control on the Toolbar can be used to select the exact magnification you wish to use with your document from 200% to 10%.

3.3

Defining Styles

In a document which has many regularly occurring pieces of text each with a different font, alignment, size or character style to the main text, it can be wearying to alter the text each time by using buttons on the Toolbar and altering the Ruler. Wouldn't it be so much easier to set up a number of styles which could be accessed in one easy move? The **Style** command enables you to do this.

- Type in a piece of text and format it exactly as you wish the style to be.

- Choose the **Style** command from the **Format** menu and in the dialogue box presented click on the **New** button. In following dialogue box enter a name for the style and click on **OK**. Click on **Close** in the **Style** dialogue box.

Now every time you wish to use that style click on the arrow to the right of the **Style Box** on the Toolbar and select the style. One style can be defined for the main text and another for the titles etc.

Normal	⬇

The style box initially displays "Normal" since this is the default style.

Using styles has another major advantage. If you have defined a particular style throughout your document and decide to change it, it's easy:

- Make all the changes you require to the style of one piece of text.

- Select the piece of text.

- Choose the current style name from the Style box.

- A dialogue box will be presented asking if you wish to **Re-define the Style Based on the Selection**. Click on **Yes**. This will re-define all instances of the style throughout your document.

Note: If you intend to include a Table of Contents in your document you may find constructing it simpler if you use Heading 1, 2 and 3 as the names for your different levels of heading styles.

Style Gallery

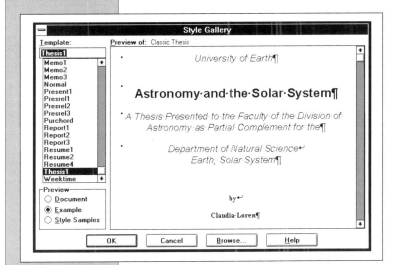

Word provides a large selection of pre-defined styles as templates. Using one of these can save time experimenting.

To display the style templates available choose **Style Gallery** from the **Format** menu. The following dialogue box is presented.

From the left of the dialogue box the style template can be chosen, on the right is a preview of the template style imposed on the document currently open. The type of preview can be changed to show a pre-defined example of the text. Clicking on **OK** will add the styles from the template to your document.

Note: Styles from the Style Gallery are not automatically imposed on your text. Use these styles as any other.

3.4 Tables

Quite often data needs to be included in a document in the form of a table. Word allows you to create tables easily. A table is a series of rows and columns which create a grid of cells. Between the rows and columns there are Gridlines which are non-printing separators and are there purely for guidance.

Creating a Simple Table

- Position the insertion point where the table is to be inserted.

- To create a simple table click on the ▦ button in the Toolbar. A pop-up menu is displayed which shows a grid of squares that represent the cells of the table you wish to create. Click and drag across this grid to specify the size of the table that you wish to create. As you do this, cells will be highlighted and the size of the table will be shown. The grid displays only 5 cells across and 4 cells down but drag beyond this and the grid will expand accordingly. Release the mouse button to create the table.

Each cell and row has a non-printing ¤ character inside for guidance.

- Type text into the cells. You can move across a row by pressing the **TAB** (→|) key or by using the mouse and clicking.

Creating a More Complex Table

Tables which consist of more than just a simple grid of cells are created most easily by using **Table Wizard**.

- Position the insertion point where the table is to be inserted.

- To use the **Table Wizard** choose the **Insert Table** command from the **Table** menu and click on the **Wizard** button in the dialogue box displayed.

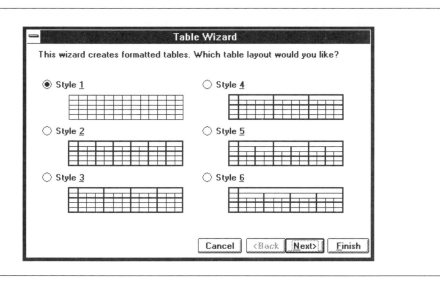

The **Table Wizard** helps you construct your table by asking a number of simple questions in a series of dialogue boxes.

- Once all the Table Wizard questions have been answered, click on the **Finish** button, the **Table AutoFormat** dialogue box will be displayed. Use this dialogue box to choose the shading and borders you wish to apply to the table. On the left of the dialogue box pre-set formats are listed. The effect of using any of these formats can be seen in the preview.

Selecting Within Tables

To select a particular cell it is only necessary for the insertion point to be inside the cell.

To select a row of cells click to the left of the first cell of the row. To select more than one row click and drag from the left of the first cell of the row down to the last row you wish to select.

To select columns of cells move the pointer to the gridline above the first column of the selection. The pointer should change to a downward pointing arrow (see below). Hold down the mouse button, drag across the columns you wish to select, and release the mouse button when your selection is complete.

To select a discrete area of cells click and drag across the range of cells.

To select the entire table ensure that the insertion point is in a cell of the table and choose **Select Table** from the **Table** menu.

Editing the Table

To delete a row or column of cells select them and then choose **Delete Columns/Rows** from the **Table** menu. Likewise to delete an entire table, select it and choose the **Delete Columns/ Rows** from the **Table** menu.

To insert a row or column select a similar row or column and choose **Insert Columns/Rows** from the **Table** menu. Alternatively, if you wish to insert another row at the foot of a table, move the insertion point to the final cell of the last row and press the **TAB** (→|) key. This will insert one identical row.

To alter the width of a column click and drag the table boundary to the required position.

Alternatively, double-click on the column boundary to have it resize automatically to the size of the data contained in the table.

If you find that moving the boundary of one column also moves another hold down the **Shift** (⇑) key while dragging.

To alter the width of a selection of the columns of your table, select the columns and then click and drag the column boundary as above.

To specify the exact size of a row or column, select the required cells and choose the **Cell Height and Width** command from the **Table** menu. Enter the cell width and height into the dialogue box presented.

Borders can be placed around the table (see Section 2.22).

Table Alignment

The contents of cells can be aligned within their cells by using the usual alignment buttons on the Toolbar.

To align the table horizontally on the page ensure that the insertion point is within the table and choose **Cell Height and Width** from the **Table** menu. From the dialogue box presented click on the **Row** tab and select the alignment you require. Click on **OK** to align the table.

Banner Headings

To join a number of cells to create a banner heading, as below, select the cells concerned and choose **Merge Cells** from the **Table** menu. You can now type in your banner heading.

To remove the banner heading select the merged cells and choose **Split Cells** from the **Table** menu.

Splitting a Table

To split a table in two choose move the insertion point to where you wish to split the table and choose the **Split Table** command from the **Table** menu.

3.5 Footnotes and Endnotes

For essays, chapters and reports the use of Footnotes or Endnotes adds precision and sophistication to your work. The distinction between footnotes and endnotes is that footnotes appear at the bottom of the page on which they are referenced whereas endnotes appear at the end of the document or the end of a section within the document. If you wish you may use both in a single document.

To insert a footnote or endnote in the text, place the insertion point where you wish the reference to appear and choose the **Footnote** command from the **Insert** menu. From the dialogue box presented choose whether you wish to use a footnote or endnote and the type of reference mark you wish to use. By default the reference mark is a number which updates with each additional note. The default numbering system is 1,2,3 for footnotes and i,ii,iii for endnotes.

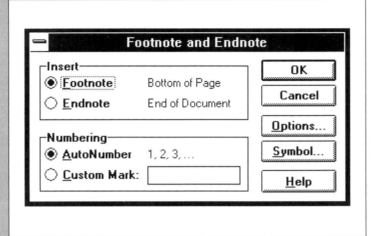

Clicking on **OK** divides the window in two separate scrollable parts and the chosen superscripted reference mark, eg. ^{1} or ^{i}, is placed just before the insertion point. The top half of the window is for you to continue to work on your main text; the bottom half of the window is for footnote or endnote text. You will notice that the same superscripted reference marker is automatically put here ready for you to type in your note. If you have used an automatic reference numbering as your reference marker and later in your text you insert another note this will be updated eg. to ^{2} or ^{ii} and the same number will be seen in the bottom part of the window under your first note.

If you decide to add a footnote in between existing footnotes, the numbering of **ALL** the footnotes will be revised automatically. The same is true of endnotes.

By default endnotes appear at the end of the document. To change this so that they appear at the end of a section choose **Footnote** from the **Insert** menu and click on the **Options** button. From the dialogue box presented choose the **Endnote** tab and choose the position of the endnote by clicking on the arrow alongside **Place At**. For more information about sections see Section 3.6.

To customise the footnote or endnote marker, from the Footnote and Endnote dialogue box click on the **Custom Mark** button and enter the required mark; to enter characters not available from the keyboard click on the **Symbol** button and choose a symbol from the dialogue box displayed. To alter the numbering system used, click on the **Options** button, from the dialogue box choose the **Footnote** or **Endnote** tab and then select the required number format.

To remove the split in the window, but not the notes themselves, click on the **Close** button at the top of the bottom section of the window. To view the footnote/endnote window choose **Footnotes** from the **View** menu or double-click on a reference marker.

Deleting Footnotes and Endnotes

To delete a footnote or endnote all that is necessary is for you to select the reference marker in the main text window and press the **Backspace** (←) key. This will delete your footnote or endnote text, reference marker and automatically re-number all remaining notes.

3.6

Re-arranging Numbered Footnotes and Endnotes

The easiest way to re-arrange a numbered footnote or endnote is to **Cut** and **Paste** its reference number from its old position to its new position. All other reference numbers will be automatically re-adjusted.

Changing the Style of Footnotes and Endnotes

Footnote text is automatically formatted in 10-point characters whilst the references are superscripted 10-point. These can be altered by re-defining the **Footnote text** and **Endnote text** default style.

Dividing Your Document into Sections

There are occasions when it would be useful to divide a document into different sections and for each section to have a different layout – headers, footers, page numbering, orientation etc.

Creating Sections

Normally your document will consist of only one section. To divide the document into sections you need to add a **Section Break**.

*   Position the insertion point where you want the new section to start.

*   Choose **Break** from the **Insert** menu. From the dialogue box presented select where you want the section break to appear. Click on **Next Page** to start the new section on a new page; click on **Continuous** if you do not wish to start a new page. A double-dotted line will appear across the screen to show that the document is separated into sections.

By default new sections have the same layout as the previous section. To change the layout of the new section move the insertion point to somewhere with in it and change the layout as below.

The following formats can be changed independently for each section:

Page Numbers – **Page Numbers** command from the **Insert** menu. See Section 3.1.

Headers/Footers – **Header/Footer** command from the **View** menu See Section 3.1.

Number of Columns – By clicking on the ▦ button on the Toolbar a pop-up menu appears. Click and drag across the sample in the pop-up menu until you have selected the number of columns you wish your section to have.

Page Orientation and Page Margins – By choosing the **Page Setup** command from the **Format** menu a dialogue box is presented. Change the **Apply to** box in the right hand corner of the dialogue box so that it reads **This Section**. To alter the margin settings for your section specify your requirements in the boxes provided. To alter the page orientation for your section click on the **Paper size** tab and make your selection.

To alter where you want the section to appear choose the **Section Layout** command from the **Format** menu and from the dialogue box that is presented the start of the section break can be changed.

To remove a section break, move the insertion point to just before the first character of the new section and press the **Backspace** (←) key.

3.7

Super^{script}
Sub_{script}

Subscript, Superscript and Large text

It is quite common to wish to use Superscript or Subscript in text. To do this, first select the piece of text you wish subscripted or superscripted. Choose the **Font** command from the **Format** menu. From the dialogue box displayed click on the superscript or subscript box.

Often you will wish superscripted or subscripted text to be smaller than the main text and you can select or type any point size into the **Size** box. In the same way if you wish particularly large text, up to 1638 points!, this is where to type in your preference.

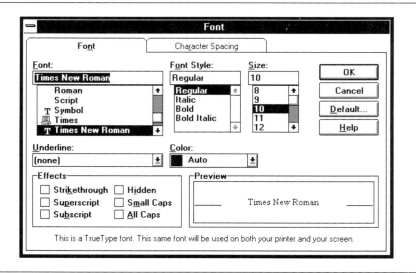

3.8

Title Pages

Title pages by definition are different to most of your document. Often title, author and other details are positioned to create an impression, and whether your title page has text, tables or graphics, each must be inserted into a **Frame**.

- Type and insert all the parts of your title page in to the first page of your document.

- As required, change the font, character style and size of any text but do not alter it's alignment. Alter the size of any graphics as required.

- Ensure that between each part of the title page you have pressed the **Enter** (↵) key twice (if paragraph markers are turned on you should see parts separated by two ¶ markers).

- Select one of the parts of the title page that you wish to position. This can include one of the ¶ markers.

- Choose the **Frame** command from the **Insert** menu and if you are viewing in Normal view a dialogue box will be presented asking if you wish to switch to **Page Layout View** (see Viewing Section 3.2) click on **No**. A non-printing box will be drawn around your selection indicating the presence of the frame.

- Repeat the above until all of the parts have been framed.

- Choose **Page Layout** from the **View** menu (see Viewing Section 3.2) to provide an overall view of the page showing all the parts of the title page enclosed in boxes.

- Move the pointer to the border of one of these boxes until the pointer shape changes to ⊕. Now the box can be clicked and dragged into position on the page.

- Repeat this for all of the parts of the title page.

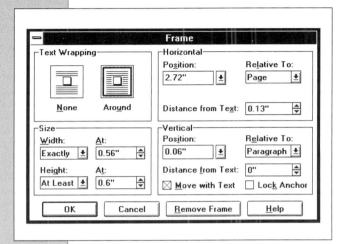

- If a frame needs to be positioned horizontally in the centre of the page, select the framed object and choose the **Frame** command from the **Format** menu. From the dialogue box presented specify **Horizontal** positioning to be **Centre** relative to **Margin**.

- Return to normal view by choosing **Normal** from the **View** menu.

A small square is displayed in the left hand margin alongside what ever you have chosen to put in a frame. This is a non-printing character which is used to indicate the presence of special formatting.

Note: Normal view does not display any positioning of text by using frames.

- A border is automatically put around all framed objects, to remove this click on the **Border** command in the **Format** menu and from the dialogue box presented click on the **None** button, and then on **OK**.

To delete it, click within the frame and from the **Format** menu choose **Frame**. Click on the **Remove Frame** button.

Remember, if you have set up headers and footers for your document, unless you specify otherwise, these will also be printed on the title page. See Section 3.1 for information on special page numbering.

3.9 Tables of Contents

When you produce a long document it is common practice to include a Table of Contents.

Constructing a Table of Contents Automatically

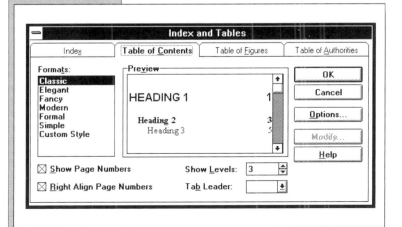

Word constructs a table of contents automatically by using text from the document formatted with styles which have been previously defined as headings. To use this method, styles for headings must have been defined. See Section 3.3. If heading styles have not been defined use the manual method described below.

- Move the insertion point to where you wish the TOC to appear.

- Choose **Index and Tables** from the **Insert** menu and from the dialogue box presented click on the **Table of Contents** tab.

- Choose the format you require for your TOC. Your choice will be previewed in the centre of the dialogue box.

- Click on the **Options** button and enter the appropriate TOC level along side the style of your choice. Delete the TOC levels alongside the default heading styles ie. Heading 1...3.

- Click on the **OK** button and the TOC will be inserted into your text at the insertion point.

- You may wish to insert a page break under the TOC to separate it from the main text.

Problem? A dialogue box is displayed which says 'Word found no paragraphs with heading styles to include in the TOC' and the words 'Error no table of contents entries found' is inserted into your text.

Solution: Ensure that you have matched the heading styles to a level in the TOC. Delete the error which appears in your text.

Automatically Updating a Table of Contents

A TOC cannot be automatically updated if it was created manually.

To update the TOC move the insertion point to within the TOC, choose **Index and Tables** from the **Insert** menu and click on **OK**. You will be presented with a dialogue box asking if you wish to replace the selected TOC. Click on the **OK** button and the TOC will be updated.

Constructing a Table of Contents Manually

Hint: Before you construct the TOC manually make sure that you have made all the last minute additions to your document because any additions after the TOC has been constructed will almost certainly make it inaccurate.

- Go through the document and write down the page numbers where the contents entries are.

- Set up a right aligned tab to the point where you wish the page numbers to align.

- Type in each contents entry manually, press the **TAB** (→|) key after each entry, and type in its page number.

- To put dotted lines between the contents entry and its page number, select the whole TOC, and choose **Tabs** from the **Format** menu.

- Click on the **2 ....** leader button and **OK**.

3.10 Tables of Figures

When you produce a long document containing many tables, illustrations and graphs it is common practice to include a Table of Figures (TOF).

Constructing a Table of Figures From a Style

If you have already provided a caption for figures and have defined a style for this purpose follow the method below otherwise see *Constructing a Table of Figures Using Captions*.

- Move the insertion point to where you wish the TOF to appear and choose **Index and Tables** from the **Insert** menu. From the dialogue box presented click on the **Table of Figures** tab.

- Choose the format you require for your TOF. Your choice will be previewed in the centre of the dialogue box.

- Click on the **Options** button, and from the dialogue box presented click on the **Style** box and choose the style you used to label your figures. Click on **OK**. Next, click on **OK** in the **Index and Tables** dialogue box and your TOF will appear in your text at the insertion point.

Constructing a Table of Figures Using Captions

- Select each figure in turn and choose **Caption** from the **Insert** menu.

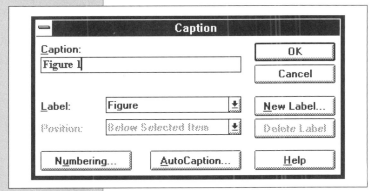

- From the dialogue box presented choose the type of label and numbering scheme you wish for your figure. By default the label *Figure* is used with the *1,2,3...* numbering scheme. Click on **OK**.

- When all figures have been captioned move the insertion point to where you wish the TOF to appear and choose **Index and Tables** from the **Insert** menu. From the dialogue box presented click on the **Table of Figures** tab.

- Choose the format you require for your TOF, and your choice will be previewed in the centre of the dialogue box.

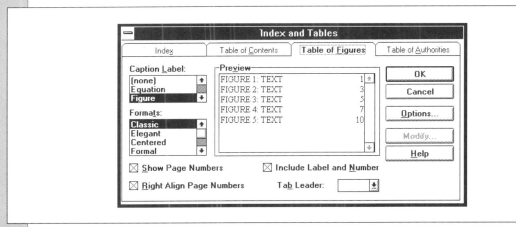

- Click on the **OK** button and the TOF will appear in your text at the insertion point.

Automatically Updating a Table of Figures

A TOF can be updated using the same method as updating a TOC.

3.11 Indexes

Word provides the facility to semi-automatically generate indexes. This section will show you how you can create a simple index. More complex indexes can be generated but to do this, consult the **Microsoft Word User's Guide**.

To Create an Index:

- Scroll through your document and each time you come across text that you wish to use in your index select this text and hold down the **Alt** and **Shift** (⇑) keys while pressing the **X** key. A dialogue box will be displayed. Click on **Mark All** if you wish all incidences of the selected text throughout your document to be indexed (note this is case sensitive). Otherwise click on **Mark**. Selecting text as an index entry encloses it in a hidden non-printing reference eg. {XE "marker"} before the text which may or may not be displayed depending on whether the ¶ button shows highlighted or not.

> Hint: Remember that an index is only as good as the entries that you include.

- When you have specified all your index entries move the insertion point to where you wish to insert the index and choose **Index and Tables** from the **Insert** menu, from the dialogue box presented click on the **Index** tab.

- Choose the format you require for your Index. Your choice will be previewed in the centre of the dialogue box.

- Click on **OK** and an index will automatically be compiled for you.

Automatically Updating an Index

To update an Index move the insertion point to within the Index, choose **Index and Tables** from the **Insert** menu, and click on **OK**. You will be presented with a dialogue box asking if you wish to replace the selected Index. Click on the **OK** button and the Index will be updated.

3.12 Sorting References and Lists

It is usual for references to be listed alphabetically by author's surname at the end of an essay. This can be very time consuming to do manually. However, Word provides a **Sort** command which will do so automatically.

To sort your references by Author surname:

- Type in the references ensuring that the authors surname is the first word of each reference and that the **Enter** (↵) key is pressed at the end of each reference.

- Select all the references that you wish to sort.

- Choose the **Sorting** command from the **Table** menu.

- A dialogue box is presented; click on **OK** and your references will be sorted.

You can use the same command to sort lists provided the **Enter** (↵) key was pressed between each item to be sorted. With lists the sort dialogue box enables you to sort descending as well as ascending, numerically and by date as well as alpha-numerically.

Tables or Tabbed columns can be sorted in the same way.

3.13 Cross-References

When creating a document it is likely that you will wish to make cross-references between pages of text. Word can do this cross-referencing for you automatically. Word is capable of more complex cross-references than shown in this guide. For more information consult the **Microsoft Word User's Guide**.

Creating a Cross-Reference

- Select the text you wish to cross-reference and choose **Bookmark** from the **Edit** menu. Name the bookmark and click on **Add**.

- Move the insertion point to the location where you wish to insert the cross-reference and type any text you wish to precede it, eg. **See Section** .

- Choose **Cross-reference** from the **Insert** menu.

- From the dialogue box presented choose **Bookmark** as the type of reference and choose what you wish to insert as a reference: the page number or the bookmark text. Choose the name of the bookmark and click on **Insert**. Click on **Close** to create the cross-reference.

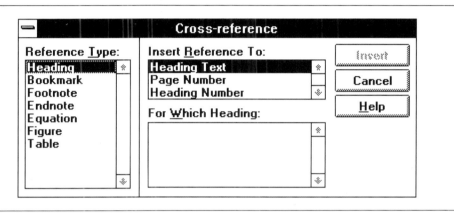

Note: To view the location of bookmarks choose the **Options** command from the **Tools** menu and select the **View** tab from the dialogue box. Click on the **Bookmarks** box and on **OK**. Bookmarked text will be seen as surrounded by greyed square brackets.

Updating and Revising Cross-References

Changes to cross-references are updated when a document is printed or Print Previewed. Deleting text which is cross-referenced will cause Word to insert an error message in the text at the reference point when the cross-references are updated. Delete the error message as any other text.

Using the Thesaurus

Word provides a Thesaurus which finds synonyms.

To use the Thesaurus:

- Select the text for which you wish to find a synonym.

- Choose the **Thesaurus** command from the **Tools** menu.

- The following dialogue box is presented with the different meanings of your selected word are displayed on the left side of the dialogue box.

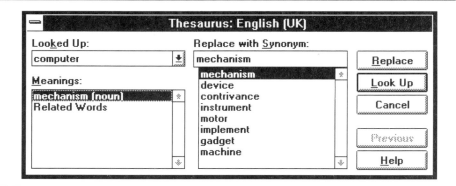

Note: It is important to remember when using a Thesaurus that words with identical spellings can have quite different meanings.

- To display the synonyms of your word click on the most appropriate meaning. The synonyms are displayed on the right side of the dialogue box.

- Click on the appropriate synonym and on the **Replace** button to change your selected text.

For further reading please see the **Microsoft Word for Windows User's Guide** which details all the commands that this booklet didn't have room for, and that's a lot believe us!

Appendix A

Using Word to Automatically Format a Document

Word provides two features which automate the creation of documents: Wizards and Templates.

Wizards

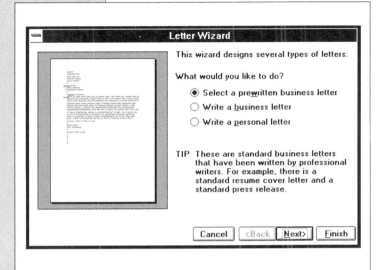

A Wizard is dedicated to the production of a particular type of document eg. a CV, a memo or a thesis. The wizard consists of a series of dialogue boxes which ask questions about the particular document. When the last question is answered Word sets up the formatting and layout of the document for you – all you need to do is type the text!

The most common wizards you are likely to use are: Letter, Memo, Newsletter, CV – Curriculum Vitae.

To use a wizard choose **New** from the **File** menu, from the dialogue box presented choose the appropriate wizard and click on **OK**. Follow the instructions as presented to create your chosen document.

Templates

Templates are pre-designed layouts for certain commonly used types of document. They differ from wizards in that questions are not asked about the formatting of the document so there is less to guide the user. The template consists of a document with several pre-defined styles along with text indicating the purpose and positioning of the style.

The most common templates you are likely to use are: Brochure, Letter, Manual, Manuscript, Memo, Presentation, Report, Resume, Thesis.

Often more than one template is included for each document type so that you can choose which is the most appropriate for your purpose.

If you know which template you wish to use choose **New** from the **File** menu, and from the dialogue box presented, choose the appropriate template and click on **OK**. Enter your own text over the bracketed text of the template.

If you would like to preview the templates available use the **Style Gallery** command from the **Format** menu. Choose the template you wish to preview and click on the **Example** button to display sample text in the template. See Section 3.3 for more information about the Style Gallery.

Note: Although creating documents in this way does take out some of the hard work if you wish to modify the formatting of the resulting document it will be necessary for you to have understood most of this guide. If you do not choose to modify the formatting there is a danger that your document will end up looking the same as everybody else's – wizards and templates are not a short-cut to learning how to use Word.

Appendix B

Creating and Inserting Graphics into your Document

Graphics can be used to great effect in a document by illustrating a point or merely by breaking up the text. Graphics can be created by use of a fully featured application, specifically for drawing or by using the drawing tool from within Word. Although not a sophisticated drawing application the drawing tool does enable you to create simple graphics and also allows you to edit graphics that have been pasted into Word.

To Create a Graphic Using the Drawing Tool

- Move the insertion point to the position in your text where you wish the graphic to appear.

- Click on the ⊡ button on the Toolbar.

- The view is switched to **Page View** and the **Drawing** Toolbar is displayed. The drawing Toolbar appears either as a standard Toolbar or as a floating Toolbar which can be dragged about the screen by its title bar.

- Click on the **Create Picture** button ⊡ on the Toolbar and draw your picture in the space provided.

Note: If the **Create Picture** button is not used, objects drawn using the draw tool overwrite or appear under text, and also they are only visible in Page View and Print Preview.

Using the Drawing Tool to Draw Objects

Anything you draw using the Tools is called an object. Several of the tools available on the Toolbar are **Geometric shapes**. To use these click on the preferred tool, move the pointer to the position on the window where you wish to start drawing, and click and drag until the shape is the desired size. When you release the mouse button the shape will be drawn.

Keep the **Shift** (⇧) key held down to draw objects symmetrically eg. a square or circle.

The **Freehand** tool is slightly different to the geometric shape tools. While the mouse button is held down a line will be drawn where ever the pointer is moved. However, when the mouse button is released and clicked elsewhere in the window a straight line is drawn between the two points. Click the mouse button when the pointer is near to where you started drawing the shape and it will be enclosed.

The **Text box** tool enables you to incorporate text into your drawing. Click at the position in the window where you wish the text to be placed and drag a rectangle to the area you wish the text to occupy. You can now type your text into the box provided.

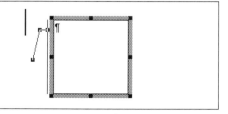

The **Callout** tool enables you to quickly incorporate text with a pointing line into your drawing. Click at the position in the window where you wish the line to point, drag to where you wish the text to be positioned and when you release the mouse button you can type the text for the callout.

Selecting Objects

To select an object click once on it's outline. By holding down the **Shift** (⇧) key objects can be selected simultaneously.

Moving Objects

To move an object:

- Select the pointer tool.

- Click once on the outline of the object.

- Click and drag one of the edges of the object (do not click and drag one of the little squares which may be present around the edge of the object).

- A dotted outline of the object will move with the pointer, and when you release the mouse button, the object will move to its new position.

Resizing Objects

- Select the pointer tool.

- Click once on the outline of the object.

- Click and drag one of the little squares or 'handles' at the corners of the object

- A dotted outline of the object will resize with the pointer, and when you release the mouse button, the object will resize.

Filling Objects

The pattern used to fill an object can be altered by selecting the object, clicking on the **Fill** tool and selecting one of the available patterns.

Line Styles

The line style used to draw the outline of an object can be altered by selecting the object, clicking on the **Line Style** tool and selecting a style from the choice available.

Text

To change the size, font and character style of text select the text, choose **Font** from the **Format** menu, and make your choice from the dialogue box displayed.

Deleting Objects

Select the object you wish to delete and choose **Clear** from the **Edit** menu.

Inserting the Graphic in Your Word Document

To insert the graphic into your document click on the **Close Picture** button.

By selecting the graphic and clicking on the 🞕 icon on the Toolbar, graphics can be positioned centrally across the page.

To resize a graphic from within Word, select it and click and drag one of the handles which appears in the corner of the graphic.

> **Problem?** When you try and position the graphic within your text it either overwrites the text or is displayed underneath it.
>
> **Solution:** The **Create Picture** [icon] button was not used before the picture was drawn. Select all the objects in the picture and click on the [icon] button. The picture may now be repositioned as above.

To Edit an Existing Graphic

Graphics that have been created using the drawing tool or pasted into Word from another application can be edited within Word.

To edit an existing graphic in your document, double-click on it, and edit using the drawing tool.

Note: To remove the drawing Toolbar from the screen choose **Toolbars** from the **View** menu, de-select the Toolbar and click on **OK**.

To Delete a Graphic

Select the graphic and press the **Backspace** (←) key.

Using Clipart

A large selection of pre-drawn artwork or Clipart is provided with Word and this can be used to good effect in enlivening the presentation of your work.

To use the clipart choose **Picture** from the **Insert** menu.

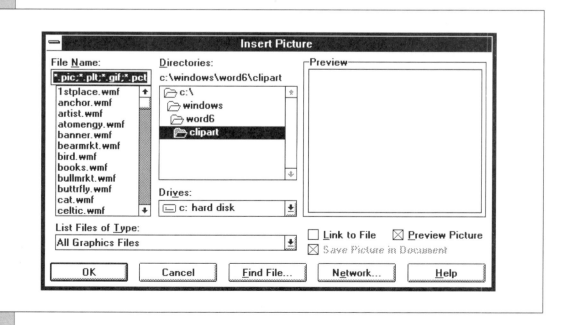

Appendix C

Creating and Inserting Charts into Your Document

Word for Windows provides an embedded application called Microsoft Graph to enable you to create simple charts.

For reasons of space, this guide will only provide the basics of how to get started using Microsoft Graph. For more information see the **Microsoft Word User's Guide**. Assistance is also provided by using the **Help** menu.

To Create a Graph Using Microsoft Graph

- Move the insertion point to the position in your text where you want the chart to appear.

- Click on the [⊞] button on the Toolbar.

- Microsoft Graph will display a window within which are two windows, the **Datasheet window** and the **Chart window**. The windows will be displayed showing the default data and chart.

The window will probably resemble the one below though with different data and chart or with no data, depending on the default set up.

HINT: Alternatively, type the data from which you wish to create a chart into a table, select it and click on the [⊞] button. This data will then be displayed in the Datasheet and a chart created in the Chart window.

The Datasheet

The chart window may be overlapping the datasheet window. If so, click on the datasheet window. To remove the default data and chart choose the **Select All** and then the **Clear** commands from the **Edit** menu. Click on **OK** in the dialogue box presented.

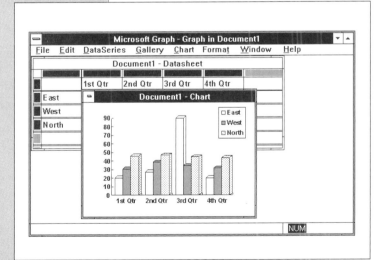

In addition to this raw data, labels are needed to describe the data in each column or row. The data in each column or row used to plot points on the graph is termed a **Data Series**, runs in columns or in rows. A double line between cells shows you which is currently selected, by default the data series is in rows. Data series in rows will create a graph with the column headings used to label an axis; data series in columns will create a graph with the row headings used to label an axis.

The datasheet is where you type in the data that will be used to create the chart. It is made up of cells which are divided into rows and columns. Data is typed into the cells of the datasheet.

To type data into a cell move the pointer to the cell, click the mouse button, and type.

Move to another cell either by using the mouse and clicking on the cell or by pressing the **Enter** (↵) key to move one cell down or by pressing the **TAB** (→|) key to move one cell to the right.

To edit the data in a cell move the pointer to the cell, click the mouse button, and edit the data in the same way as you edit text in Word.

Cells can be selected by clicking and dragging. You can click and drag horizontally, vertically and diagonally. To select an entire column of cells click on the shaded cell above the column; to select an entire row of cells click on the shaded cell to the left of the row.

To insert rows or columns select the row or column where you want to make the insertion and choose **Insert Row/Column**. To delete a row or columns choose **Delete Row/Column**.

Microsoft Graph allows you to change the format of the data that you type by choosing **Number** from the **Format** menu. By default the Number format is the same as you type.

Creating a Chart From Your Data

As you type data into the Datasheet a chart is automatically created in the Chart window using the default chart format (probably column chart).

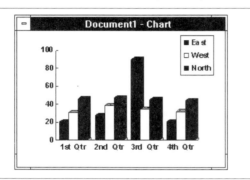

To change the chart type, click on the Chart window and choose the type of chart that you wish from the **Galley** menu.

By choosing one of the chart types a chart will be created from the Datasheet. If you want to try another format for your chart choose the appropriate command from the **Gallery** menu. The **Combination** command will overlay one chart type upon another.

Editing the Chart

The extent to which you can edit chart text depends on whether the text is attached to a particular part of the chart or unattached. Examples of **Attached text** are the labelling of the axes and chart titles, neither of which can be moved. Attached text can be edited by double-clicking and typing in the dialogue box provided.

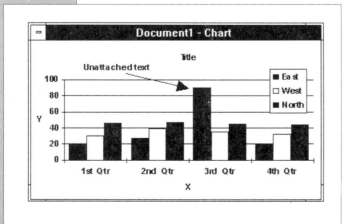

To add unattached text ensure that no other text is selected and begin typing. Unattached text can be moved around the chart by clicking and dragging. Like attached text double-click on it to edit the text.

To change the alignment and orientation of any text, select the text and choose the **Text** command from the **Format** menu, choose the appropriate options from the dialogue box presented.

To format either axis double-click on it and choose the appropriate options from the dialogue box presented.

Arrows can be added by choosing the **Add Arrow** command from the **Chart** menu. The position of the arrow can be altered by clicking and dragging on the centre of the arrow, and the length and angle of the arrow can be altered by clicking and dragging on one of its ends.

A legend is added automatically to your chart. The legend provides a key to the symbols and patterns used to represent the data on the chart. It can be repositioned by clicking and dragging.

Gridlines can be added to the chart by choosing the **Gridlines** command from the **Chart** menu and clicking on the appropriate options in the dialogue box presented.

To delete any of the components of the chart select the component and press the **Backspace** (←) key.

To alter the fill pattern of column or bar charts double-click on the column or bar showing the pattern you wish to alter. Select a new pattern from the dialogue box presented. Likewise, to alter the plot symbol double-click on the plot symbol and select an alternative from those provided.

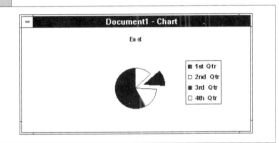

When using a Pie chart each section of pie can be clicked and dragged to provide emphasis.

For 3D charts a special **3D-View** command is provided, this is available from the **Format** menu.

Inserting the Chart

To insert the chart into your document choose the **Exit and Return** command from the **File** menu, if asked whether to update graph, click on **Yes**. The chart will be inserted and when you save your document the chart and the data you typed in to create it will also be saved in the same file.

Appendix D

Creating and Inserting Formulae into your Document

An **Equation Editor** is provided as part of Word and this enables you to build complex equations into your text.

For reasons of space, this guide will only provide the basics of how to get started using the Equation Editor. For more detail see the Microsoft Word User's Guide or the **Help** menu.

To create an equation in your document, move the insertion point to where you wish the equation to appear and from the **Insert** menu choose **Object**. A dialogue box will appear. Choose **Microsoft Equation 2.0** from the list displayed and then click on **OK**. A shaded rectangle appears in your text, the Equation Toolbar is displayed, and the menus change on the menu bar.

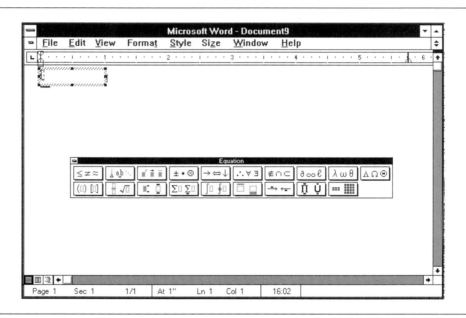

An equation is composed of Templates, Symbols and Keyboard characters each of which is inserted into **Slots**. An empty slot can be identified by a dotted box and such a slot is displayed each time the equation editor window is opened.

Templates themselves have slots into which symbols, keyboard characters or even other templates can be inserted.

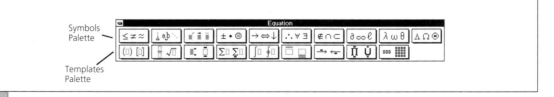

Symbols Palette

Templates Palette

Symbol and Template Palettes

The Equation Editor window has its own menu bar and two palettes: the **Template palette** and the **Symbol palette**. The palettes provide quick and easy access to the components of an equation which are not available from the keyboard.

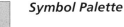

Symbol Palette

This palette displays some of the most common symbols which you are likely to use in your equation, and by clicking on one of these symbols a pop-up menu is displayed from which you can choose related symbols.

Some symbols, called embellishments, are shown on the menu consist of a partly greyed slot. This indicates that the symbol chosen will appear as part of the previous character. For example, to achieve the character $\bar{e}$: type the variable e and from the embellishment symbols palette select ▓. The bar will appear on top of the e.

Characters from the Symbol palette can also be embellished in this way.

Template Palette

This palette displays some of the most commonly used mathematical relationships which you are likely to use as part of your equation. By clicking on one of these templates a pop-up menu is displayed from which you can choose related templates.

Some templates display their slots as dotted boxes, others as filled boxes. A template which contains dotted slots will be drawn full size; templates with filled slots will be drawn scaled to fit the equation.

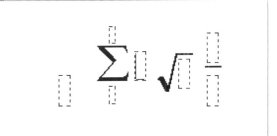

Whichever type of slot the template has, each slot must be filled in to complete the template.

The size of each component of the equation is adjusted automatically for you following typesetting conventions. To change the size of any of the components of the equation refer to the **Microsoft Word User's Guide** or use the **Help** menu.

By default, any character which the Equation Editor recognises as a mathematical variable is displayed in Italic. Until you have completed typing a function, such as **sin**, it, too, is displayed as italic. On completion it will be recognised as a function and displayed in plain Times Roman.

Note: The above is case sensitive so typing *Sin* will cause the equation editor to assume you are using a variable where as typing *sin* will cause it to assume a function.

There is no need to press the **Space Bar** in the Equation Editor as spacing is automatically adjusted.

To create equations that are piled one upon another press the **Enter** (↵) key between equations. These equations can be aligned by selecting the equation and choosing the required alignment from the **Format** menu.

The Insertion Point

The insertion point in the Equation Editor is **L** shaped so as to allow more precise positioning within equations.

To move the insertion point on to the next slot press the **TAB** (→|) key or use the mouse. Pressing the **Shift** (⇑) key at the same time as **TAB** will move the insertion point back a slot.

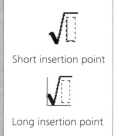

Short insertion point

Long insertion point

The size of the insertion point changes depending on which slot it is in. The vertical line of the insertion point indicates the position in the slot where any insertion will appear, and the horizontal line indicates the bottom edge of the slot. If the insertion point is short and extends below only the last insertion any further insertion will be part of the preceding template. However, if the horizontal line of the insertion point is long and extends below many of the components of the equation the next insertion will be inserted after the preceding template. To make the horizontal line of the insertion point long like this move to the last slot and press the **TAB** (→|) key.

Editing an Existing Equation

The procedure for editing an equation is similar to editing text in Word though it is important to first understand how the insertion point works in the Equation Editor and how to select parts of the equation.

To edit a component of the equation use the mouse or the **TAB** (→|) key to select the slot that you wish to edit. If you select something within the slot then anything that you type will overwrite it. To alter the contents of part of the slot use the mouse to reposition the insertion point within the slot.

Once an equation has been created templates such as fences, square roots, overbars and underbars cannot easily be added. In this case to add templates such as these it is necessary to select all the components of the equation that you wish to lie underneath or on top of the template. Choose **Cut** from the **Edit** menu, and then select the fence, square root, overbar or underbar template that you wish to use from the template menu. Move the insertion point to the slot in the template and then choose **Paste** from the **Edit** menu.

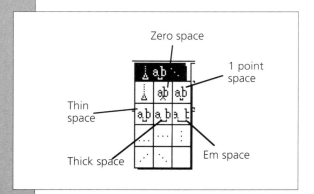

Zero space

1 point space

Thin space

Thick space

Em space

By default the Equation Editor automatically adjusts the spacing between components of the equation. However, there may be times when you wish to customise spacing. To insert extra spaces use the **Spaces/Ellipses** button from the **Symbol** palette.

The Equation Editor provides a level of control over spacing and alignment of your equation which is beyond the scope of this guide.

To delete any part of an equation select the part(s) you wish to delete then press the **Backspace** (←) key.

To insert the equation into your document click anywhere outside the grey rectangle where you defined the equation.

To resize an equation in your document click once on the equation and click and drag on one of the handles in the corner of the rectangle surrounding the equation.

To edit an equation inserted into your document double-click on the equation, the equation Toolbar will be presented and you will be able to edit as normal.

Appendix E

WordArt

WordArt provides the ability to manipulate text in fancy ways, this can be useful for headings and posters etc. Below are some examples of what WordArt can do.

To use WordArt move the insertion point to the position in your text where you wish to put a fancy graphic and choose the **Object** command from the **Insert** menu. A dialogue box will be presented, from which you select **Microsoft WordArt 2.0** and then click on **OK**. The WordArt dialogue box is then displayed.

Type your text into the text box overwriting the words **Your Text Here**. Use the menus and the Toolbar to select from the range of Fonts, Character styles, Sizes, Fills and Alignments to achieve the effect you desire. Click on **OK** when you are finished and the fancy graphic will be placed in your text.

Double-click on the graphic to edit a previously created WordArt graphic.

Appendix F

Importing and Exporting Documents

Moving data between applications is extremely useful since it allows you to mix the capabilities of Word with the specialist features of a graphics or spreadsheet application. It also avoids the labour of re-typing, or the possibility of introducing errors.

Text, numbers and graphics can be imported and exported with Word. These are referred to here collectively as data.

Importing Data

There are two ways of importing data from other applications into Word for Windows.

- By Cutting and Pasting data into Word.

- By saving the data in a format that can be opened by Word.

Cutting, and Pasting Data into Word

The way that you **Cut**, **Copy** and **Paste** between applications is more or less the same. Here is an example of how to copy data from almost any application into Word.

Select the data in the application. Choose **Copy** from the **Edit** Menu. **Exit** the application. Open Word. Select the place where you wish the data to appear, and choose **Paste** from the **Edit** menu.

Importing Saved Data

Importing data already saved has the advantage that you have a stored copy should anything go wrong. It is also the easiest way to transfer data between different types of computer, eg. PC to Macintosh.

Data from another application needs to have been saved in a format that Word for Windows can understand. There are several of these formats known variously as Text (ASCII), Word (for Windows 1,2, DOS versions 3–6, Macintosh versions 4–6), WordPerfect versions 5 series, RTF-DCA, Lotus 1-2-3 versions 2, 3, Excel versions 2–5, Windows Write.

Most applications will be capable of saving their data in one of these formats. However, be aware that importing and exporting can result in the loss of some of the characteristics of your data eg. loss of formatting in a wordprocessed document, loss of formula in a spreadsheet worksheet. Import and export using text only (ASCII) as a last resort. In most cases you will find that Word can open files without any need to resort to saving in a different file format.

The way that you import any kind of saved data into Word for Windows is more or less the same.

- First any data exported to be imported should be saved as normal provided the format is one of those listed above. Alternatively save as text.

- **Exit** the application and open Word for Windows.

- Select **Open** from the **File** menu. This will present a dialogue box. Click on the arrow to **List Files of Type** and choose **All Files (*.*)**. Select the file you wish to import and click on **Open**. The file will be converted into Word for Windows format.

Importing Data from a Macintosh Application

Most data saved on a Macintosh computer can be imported into Word for Windows.

The basic procedure is the same as above except that the disc used to save the file on must be in PC disc format. The **Apple File Exchange** program supplied with every Macintosh can be used to create such a disc. Seek assistance if you do not know how to use this program. Save the file on the disc and open the file from Word for Windows as described above. Depending on the choice of font used in the original data you may find that an alternative has been substituted by Word for Windows and that this changes the appearance of your document.

> If the file name on the Macintosh was longer than 8 characters the file name on the PC will be contracted to 7 characters and an ampersand (&). If spaces were used in the Macintosh file name the spaces will be not be shown on the PC.

Exporting Data

There are two ways of exporting data to another application from Word for Windows.

- By copying and pasting data.
- By using saved data.

Using Copy and Paste

This method will only work for exporting to other Windows applications.

Select the data which you wish to export and **Copy** it. Close Word for Windows. **Open** the application to which you wish to export the data. Move the insertion point to where you wish the data to appear and choose **Paste** from the **Edit** menu.

Using Saved Data

This is the only way to export data to non-Windows PC applications and applications on other computers eg. Macintosh, but it can also be useful to transfer between Windows applications too.

Open the document which you wish to export. Choose the **Save As** command from the **File** menu. Click on the arrow alongside the **Save File As Type** box and select the file type that you know can be imported by your application (see above for full list). Open the file as normal.

> Remember: not all formats save all the information contained in a Word for Windows file. Text (ASCII) for example will not save any formatting. So make sure that you keep a copy of the document in normal Word for Windows format.

Exporting Data to a Macintosh Application

Most data saved on an PC can be exported to a Macintosh application.

The basic procedure is the same as above except that before the files can be opened they must be transferred to the Macintosh using the **Apple File Exchange** program supplied with every Macintosh. Seek assistance if you do not know how to use this program. Once transferred the file can be opened from the Macintosh application as normal. Depending on the choice of font used in the original data you may find that an alternative has been substituted by Word for Macintosh and that this changes the appearance of your document.

Notes...